Personal Certainty

On the Way, the Truth, & the Life

VALENTIN TOMBERG

Personal Certainty
On the Way, the Truth, & the Life

(Seed · Seed-Force · Tree)

Foreword by
Friederike Migneco
Volker Zotz

Preliminary Note by
Therese Schroeder-Sheker

 Angelico Press

For information, address:
Angelico Press
169 Monitor St.
Brooklyn, NY 11222
angelicopress.com

ISBN 978-1-62138-897-5 (pbk)
ISBN 978-1-62138-898-2 (cloth)

Cover Design: Michael Schrauzer

TABLE OF CONTENTS

Preliminary Note

by Therese Schroeder-Sheker

ROM ANTIQUITY TO THE PRESENT, IN TRIBUNALS large and small, the most risk-oriented leaders have often been reduced, misquoted, besmirched, or maligned. Those risking the cutting edge have frequently been dismissed, buried, or declared anathema for reasons that make later generations wince. Only when these inner Argonauts are safely dead and gone does history tend to lift and laud them, at which point even the encrusted institutions embrace them. Front-runners are never theorists or abstractionists. They are individuals who valiantly grapple with reality, who search and discover, see and hear, experience and encounter, then write or speak of that with which they have had direct contact and intimate experience.

Like the many historical sojourners who have suffered exile, whether from within the sciences or the humanities, Valentin Tomberg has at times also suffered cultural disfigurement: the disfigurement of interpretation, the disfigurement of misinterpretation, the disfigurement of detraction. None of the three processes are neutral; each can mar, color, and skew. For these reasons, the publication of each of Tomberg's major writings is another victory, allowing his companion readers to ignore distractions and go directly to the source if they want to learn what it was that Tomberg truly said and thought. By shouldering the grappling efforts

i

individually rather than outsourcing our efforts to others, in other words by reading him directly rather than relying upon an interpretation or summative reconstruction of him, we first do the work ourselves, allow him to speak for himself, and afford him the dignity deserved. At that point, readers can freely come to their own conclusions and along the way, discover a bonus: they have taken another step forward towards individuation.

Personal Certainty strikes me as a work of astonishing maturity, humility, texture, and insight. It maps the human-making curriculum required of and inhabited by a specific writer of consummate merit and unique destiny. Tomberg consistently moved forward—evolved—through internal and external experience of war and upheaval, turbulence and concentration, migration and choice, ideals and possibilities, hope and disappointment, truth and deception, strength and fragility, hypocrisy and integrity. Most of all, he was able to share intimately regarding the mystery of prayer, meditation, contemplation, liturgy, the rosary, while reflecting upon the communion of saints, the Risen Christ, Mary and all that is Sophianic, and more. As his perspectives widened and deepened, *Certainty* traces how and why new capacities rooted and were liberated in his life and how he sustained human, intellectual, psychological, and spiritual growth. In tracing how he learned to diagnose personal error, how he learned to change, how he found the courage to reconsider his personal religious commitment, how he learned to re-adjust and self-correct, we learn of the consciousness required to actually inhabit and shoulder freedom in a new and living way. Were he here today, he would face similar difficulties, requiring other conscious and costly "free" decisions, each heroic, valoric, and loving. Since history has labeled this the post-truth era, the testimony of one man's *Personal Certainty* could not be more urgently needed. As such, it is sacred medicine.

THERESE SCHROEDER-SHEKER
Chalice of Repose Project

Foreword on "Personal Certainty"

by Friederike Migneco
and Volker Zotz

 N THE FEAST OF THE ASSUMPTION IN 1956, VAL-
entin Tomberg began to work on the hitherto
unpublished text which is set before the reader
in this book. Preliminary sketches for it are doc-
umented as dating from the previous year, among which is a
partial study entitled "On the Nature of Symbolism."[1] The
typescript on which this edition is based is superscribed
with the date March 18, 1957.

Originally, Tomberg envisaged calling the planned book
Science, Philosophy, Religion—and Truth; later he considered
calling it *The Seed, the Seed-Force, the Tree: A Contribution to
the Problem of the Way, the Truth, and the Life*, or, alterna-
tively, *On the Sources of Personal Certainty*.[2] The English edi-
tor has chosen the primary title *Personal Certainty: On the
Way, the Truth, and the Life*, to bring together the intentions
at the bottom of the various ideas its author had envisaged.

Written in the second half of Tomberg's life (a decade or
so following his conversion to Catholicism), this text docu-
ments an essential, transitional stage in the development of
his work. Here Tomberg gives an account of how far, and in

---

[1] Cf. Elisabeth Heckmann and Michael Frensch, *Valentin Tomberg*, Vol. I.2
(Schaffhausen: Novalis Verlag, 2005), 286ff.

[2] Ibid.

what way, he might be truly *certain* of matters pertaining to the great questions humanity faces. These questions, "which are like hunger and thirst," concern the "origin and destiny of the world, the ruling principle or nature of the world, the nature of human personhood, its fate and its calling in life and in death." (45) Tomberg's essay thus aims at nothing less than at personal certainty about the ultimate issues, a certainty whose contents it would not be possible to dismiss as "just another" disputed set of opinions over what is held to be true. Yet for him it was a matter of much greater consequence than becoming personally certain himself of having reached an unassailable vantage point. He wanted to discover and set out the *method* by means of which other seekers might also arrive at authentic certainty regarding the great questions.

The claim thus made of having shown a path to authentic knowledge, of truth (a path, of course, that must be trodden on one's own, but even so could be understood by others and thus claim a quasi-objective validity), might with some justice be considered as a presumptuous one. Tomberg may himself have seen that perhaps he had set the bar for his project too high, for after some introductory remarks to chapter six, he broke off work on this text, which he had originally considered as his "life's work." But even if he did not bring it to a close, this work offers invaluable glimpses into Tomberg's workshop: into his method of uncovering insights into truth by contemplating symbols, and into the way he pursued his thoughts.

⊕

In order to understand at least in part what led Tomberg to risk, in this book, such an audacious experiment with what he called the "total method," we need to take a look at the era in which he lived, and at some significant stages of his spiritual development.

Born in St. Petersburg in 1900, Tomberg grew up in an intellectual climate in which, in Europe, the results and thought-patterns of the triumphant natural sciences were more and more invoked to explain many aspects in all areas of life. In this atmosphere, assertions could be held to be valid if they were based on what was known to biology, chemistry, or physics; or if, at least, they were deduced from such knowledge. When zoologist Ernst Haeckel translated the Judeo-Christian idea of a spiritual God (hidden from the senses and whose likeness was the human being) into the image of a "gaseous vertebrate," to many, that former idea of God seemed to have become obsolete. Then Marxism stepped forward as a "scientific socialism" widely believed to be able to foresee the necessary phases of the future development of the economy and of political history on the basis of its knowledge of the laws of matter.

The young Tomberg, who by the time he reached puberty had already been deeply engaged with the Russian Orthodox faith, was among those of his generation who could not accept that the reasonings of the natural sciences were adequate for all areas of culture, or for the life of the spirit and of the soul. Without calling into doubt the significance of discoveries in biology and physics in their own domains, Tomberg harbored no expectation that they would be able to decide questions about the origin, meaning, and goal of the world or of human existence. He wished to follow other paths towards questions of the spirit than those suitable to the investigation of matter.

When he was seventeen, Tomberg joined the Theosophical Society, having turned already previously towards the teachings of Russian and French Hermeticists, for whom traditional symbols drawn from alchemy, astrology, and the kabbalah were essential sources of knowledge.

The interpretation of symbols remained a priority for Tomberg, and one with which he was also deeply concerned in the present text. Yet in the longer run, the method of the Hermeticists did not satisfy him. Yes, interpretative meditation upon symbols may assist in the individual clarification of questions about one's worldview and about how to live, but it can easily lead down a false trail into a labyrinth of private mythologies. In this latter case, instead of making reality more comprehensible, symbolism can lead to its mystification: rather than what is hidden coming to light, obvious things are veiled. If Hermeticism were to branch off into such a labyrinth, it would prove to be as one-dimensional as natural science.

In its concentration on the material world, and in its purely logical concern with facts, science remains confined to the sphere of the objective, in which it cannot do justice to subjective questions that arise "like hunger and thirst." On the other hand, a Hermetic method that has wandered too far into the domain of private mythologies yields results that elude universal verification: their value remains purely subjective. If, from the perspective of a search for meaning, we may say that natural science remains on the surface, then, even though an Hermetic approach most surely does descend into the depths, it may equally be said that it runs the risk of getting lost in mysterious speculations for want of any possibility of objective verification.

⊕

From the 1920s onwards, it seemed to Tomberg that a way out of this dilemma (in which one can either have certain but superficial results, or descend into the depths at the risk of losing one's way) was afforded by Anthroposophy, for Rudolf Steiner's teaching claimed to be a *"science of the spirit."* The results of anthroposophical research were supposed to be replicable (just like those of natural science) if the same research protocol was repeated. Accordingly, in his book, *Knowledge of the Higher Worlds and Its Attainment*, Steiner writes thus about research into what lies beyond birth and death:

> Anyone can acquire this knowledge; everyone has the ability to know for himself, to see for himself [...] it is only a question of choosing the right means.

That Steiner won over many intellectuals and artists to his conception of a purportedly scientific investigation of the supersensible was owed not least to the fact that he knew how to make his inner experiences productive in the arts, in Waldorf schools, and in biodynamic agriculture. Undeniably, Steiner's inner, spiritual research led to powerful outer, objective effects. But as far as "knowledge of the higher worlds" was concerned, anthroposophists (for the most part) refrained from attempting to *test* the results communicated by Steiner. Instead of "knowing for oneself, seeing for oneself," disputes arose among many of Steiner's followers, especially after his death, over the correct "exegesis" of what Steiner himself had experienced and reported in his vast body of work. That work came to be treated more as a "deposit of faith" than as a stimulus to further research on the part of *others* coming after him.

Those few who, like Tomberg, *did* carry out spiritual research in the 1930s, and who claimed, like Steiner, to have access to insights into spheres beyond the sense-perceptible, reached widely different results. Unfortunately, Tomberg was to discover that what *he* had to communicate as *new* results of spiritual research regarding the Old Testament (and later regarding the New Testament) was vehemently rejected by most other anthroposophists.

⊕

Now, the Catholic tradition, to which Tomberg had turned himself in the mid-1940s, emphasized, like all Christian denominations, the significance of *faith*. In the actual lives of religious people, this mostly meant (in the case of ideas not transparent to the understanding) simply *accepting* such ideas as handed down by historical or ecclesiastical authorities. The Tomberg who had been formed by Rudolf Steiner's work could not, however, adopt this prevailing position. His decision in favor of Catholicism was in no way a decision *against* knowledge. Therefore, he distanced himself unambiguously from Martin Luther's *sola fide,* for in that idea there vanished from religion not only

> the principle of actually *practicing* a religion . . . and thus of the practice of the rosary, spiritual exercises in the sense of meditation and contemplation, the examination of one's conscience, confession, the vows of poverty, obedience, and chastity—but it was also tantamount to renouncing also the principle of gnosis that underlies this practice. It meant renouncing the principle of striving to become worthy of suprasensory and suprarational illumination and insight by means of preparatory instruction. (159–60)

Foreword on "Personal Certainty"

The Failure of the "Total" Method

In the present text, Tomberg was seeking an understanding of faith that would allow him to do justice to the teachings of the Church, *without relinquishing his desire for knowledge.* For Tomberg, belief in the Christian sense could not merely mean accepting one of many competing views.

> Faith is not an opinion upon which one insists, but is instead like the imprinting of a seal on the whole of a person's consciousness, which is made good by its *weight.* (136)

If the contents of belief embrace "the whole of a person's consciousness," then the aspect of knowledge in that consciousness cannot simply be bracketed out. That which is supposed to have "weight" for the whole of one's life must also, in the deepest sense, be *known.* Thus, Tomberg's text can also be read as a plea for *gnosis.* It rests, in this regard, on the testimony of the gospel:

> Knowledge (for gnosis *means* knowledge), however, cannot be denied in principle if we wish to be pupils of the Master who commanded us: "Know the truth, and the truth shall make you free." (157)

Starting from this premise, Tomberg distinguishes a legitimate gnostic path from an heretical gnosis leading to dualistic doctrines:

> Alongside false gnosis can there not also exist a true gnosis, just as scientific errors exist alongside true scientific achievements? We cannot reject science outright just because there have also been, and still are, scientific errors. Should gnosis, then, as the striving for deeper insight into religious truths, be judged any

differently? Should this whole area of interest be condemned solely on the grounds that once upon a time
there were erroneous gnostic teachings? (158)

If Tomberg wanted to understand gnosis here literally as
"knowledge," it was, for him, about more than reconciling
faith and reason. This is what is meant when Pope Benedict
XVI, for example, speaks of the "connection of faith with
the searching of human reason," and (with reference to the
apostle Paul) affirms that the Christian path stands "in
accord with the eternal Word and with our reason." Tomberg, however, distinguishes "between a higher gnosis and
a rationalistically limited gnosis." (159) He understands
higher gnosis in the sense of a striving for "suprasensory
and suprarational illumination…" (160)

It is precisely in order to believe *and* to know, to know
and to understand—in order, that is, to arrive at actual personal certainty—that Tomberg in this text suggests the procedure he calls the "total" method:

> The method on which the work is based is the total
> exertion of the total human being in order to arrive at
> a total result. Hence it embraces lived experience,
> observation, study, conscience, thinking, feeling,
> guided imagination, intimations, prayers, immer-
> sion, and more. (5)

The result of this total method would consist of the harmony of the conclusions arrived at by way of various methodological paths. Tomberg illustrates this with the image of
a rainbow. That which different human capacities (such as
logic, morality, the sense for values and for beauty) all alike
accept as true, can become a *personal certainty* as the fruit of
a *total, holistic knowledge.*

Naturally, and perhaps ironically, such a total method, precisely to the extent it wishes to be *a* particular method, is condemned to fail. The individual concerned to follow it all the way would need to have at his disposal all-embracing life experience, as well as (to mention only a few aspects) the capacity for observation, for consistent thinking, for examination of conscience, for meditative deepening—all developed to such a powerful degree that the results would shine out alongside each other like the colors of the rainbow, and, as a whole, supply unshakable certainty.

If we would not wish to go so far as to dismiss this sort of realization of Tomberg's total method as a chimera on the grounds of its improbability, a better approach might be to do it justice by understanding it instead as an ideal. As an ideal, it may orient those seeking for meaning in how best to direct their activities; and, perhaps, in a few rare cases, lead them to at least provisional achievements, rather than to so lofty a goal as Tomberg had supposedly reached himself or had thought it possible for others to reach in a permanent manner.

Tomberg must have become aware of this, at the latest, by the time he broke off work on the present text, which he then refrained from publishing. As matters turned out, during Advent and Christmas of 1957 he underwent a "shattering experience of awakening," from the perspective of which his previous life came to seem a "desert" to him.[3] It was probably in the autumn of the following year that he began drafting his *Meditations on the Tarot: A Journey into Christian Hermeticism*. One result of this was that further

---

[3] See letter from Tomberg to his friend Ernst von Hippel from January 4, 1958, in Heckmann and Frensch, *Valentin Tomberg*, Vol. I.2, 309–14.

work on the personal certainty manuscript became quite definitively superfluous.[4]

The failure of the implementation of his total method, which unites science and reason with Christian belief as well as with a higher gnosis striving for illumination, distanced Tomberg from Rudolf Steiner's "spiritual-scientific" position. He no longer followed Steiner in the latter's assumption that one could achieve and objectively test knowledge of the supersensory in the same way insights into the properties of chemical elements, once ascertained, could always and everywhere be experimentally demonstrated. Insofar as the subjective certainty of "living in the truth" is a *personal* certainty, it does not make the scientific claim to be replicable by anyone who, as Rudolf Steiner had taught, "simply chooses the right means." In the draft of a letter from 1970, Tomberg formulated his reasons for rejecting Rudolf Steiner's claim to "scientificity"—a position he maintained thereafter until the end of his life:

> None of this is spiritual science. I do not mean by this, however, that there is not now, and never has been, such a thing as spiritual knowledge. I mean only that spiritual knowledge is not science, but is inner certainty, which is a state that cannot be imposed on others—at least without renouncing the claim to be universally valid and verifiable. For spiritual knowledge is based on personal experience of the most intimate sort. Thus, it can only be shared (if it is shared at all) within an intimate circle of companions, of fellow-travelers, brought together by destiny.[5]

---

[4] Ibid., 314.
[5] Ibid., 523.

Tomberg's distancing of himself from Steiner's attempt at a scientific demeanor was by no means a categorical rejection of Steiner himself, nor of all the methods and substantive positions taught by Steiner. Neither was it any sort of condemnation of Steiner, as some interpreters have thought it possible to infer. Tomberg still spoke glowingly of Steiner even at a later date,[6] although after the text on personal certainty he grew ever more distant from the claim to be able to speak of the experience of the truth in terms of a universal validity whose content could be verified by anyone choosing the right means. Accordingly, he later presented the chapters of his *Meditations on the Tarot* as Letters addressed to an "Unknown Friend." Instead of relying upon societies with codified contents accepted as binding by their members, Tomberg settled for the inspiration of individuals by individuals, of "friends" by "friends."

Power and Impotence of the Intellect

The state of renouncing "the claim to be universally valid and verifiable" that Tomberg had laid down as a prerequisite in the draft letter quoted above is made especially clear in the present text in respect of knowledge of God. Thus, for Tomberg, the attempts of Thomas Aquinas, Anselm of Canterbury, and Leibniz "to make God and God's existence compelling by means of such conceptual argument have fallen short." (118) The inconceivability of a God Who allows Himself to be reduced to nothing, appears (to the intellect) as an unreasonable demand. And yet, once it has been shown in this way to be impossible, objectively, to

[6] See Tomberg's *Proclamation on Sinai: Covenant and Commandments* (Brooklyn, NY: Angelico Press, 2022), 134–36.

establish the existence of God, it turns out that subjective experience in faith permits true openness towards Him.

Moreover, on the path to personal certainty, both a thinking that searches for proofs and a seeking faith can travel a long way together, enriching each other in such a way as to permit a person wholly to grow into truth. But in the end, the intellect arrives at the insight that it is incapable (solely out of its own resources) either of thinking or of comprehending a "wholly other" that surpasses it. In arriving at this insight, the intellect in effect admits to itself its own *impotence*—for it could only gain power over that which it would wholly comprehend.

Hence, Tomberg is not promoting any sort of "renunciation of thinking" such as he attributes to those materialistic ideas that grant *being* priority over *consciousness*—the latter being, on the contrary, always primary. (32) Because a truly consistent thinking always travels to the end of the paths open to it, such a thinking serves to prepare those in quest of personal certainty. This is why the classical proofs of God's existence—although they have "really failed"—are nonetheless necessary stations along the way. For Tomberg:

> Reason is not to be excluded or put to sleep, but to kneel in wakeful brightness before what is higher than it. It is not itself to speak, but to silently hearken. It is not to create its own forms of thinking, but to become as smooth as a mirror, and reflect. (167–68)

In the Christian tradition, one can think in this connection of the silence of Thomas Aquinas, who in the end regarded the ideas put forward in his extensive philosophical and theological work as insignificant:

> I can do no more. Everything I have written seems to me as straw in comparison with what I have seen and what has been revealed to me.

A thinking that has truly traveled "to the end of its capacity" knows that it can never force into human categories that which surpasses all that is known to us. Moreover, the use of the intellect has not been renounced simply because thought has been taken to its final possible limit. It has, rather, been freed from the delusion that it can conquer a terrain in which it is incapable of moving under its own power. In that we have not merely *abstractly known* the inconceivability of the "last things" for human beings here, but have instead *existentially experienced* the limits of thinking, we have arrived at a stance appropriate to the mystery. If reason can, in the image used by Tomberg, "kneel in wakeful brightness before what is higher" and become a mirror, the stance of humility need not mean humiliation. To the contrary, such an experience of impotence is enriching, for it allows us to become open and receptive, and thus makes us loving.

Symbol versus System

If thinking is to become truly capacious, it must not limit itself to words with defined meanings. A fixed approach of this kind narrows the knowledge to be expected from it to the radius of previously accepted definitions. If one really wishes to do justice to the "last things" by reflecting on them, one must make use of free and open media. Instead of unambiguous concepts, which lay down a definite meaning for objects of thought—and thus apparently allow those objects to be mastered—what is needed is a broader reflection on symbols, the interpretation of which can never be wholly exhausted. For Tomberg, symbols offer the only appropriate means to express and to communicate personal certainty.

A symbol makes it possible to address people "beyond the level at which their consciousness is, or was, currently awake." (22) The symbol leaves each interpreter free. It is "a path to deepening; it yields content upon content, stored in layers within it." (120) Maturing along this path

> is really the process of a series of experiences of waking up, one after another. To be mature is to be awake to the essential concerns of human life. (10)

The motif of awakening runs through the whole text: to be a person includes both sleeping layers of nocturnal consciousness that harbor wisdom *and* layers of daytime consciousness that have been shaped by reason. The harmony of both spheres is necessary in order to find and to maintain psychological and bodily health. With the help of symbols, Tomberg tells us, we can awaken still sleeping layers, so that

> *true personal certainty is the result of the agreement of the waking consciousness with the deeper, or sleeping, consciousness.* (48)

To which he then adds that he has

> been concerned with symbolism his whole life long, but to this day has never had the feeling that he has given the final interpretation of even a single symbol, i.e., that he has exhausted the content of any symbol. (121)

⊕

Since symbolism expresses subtle experiences that can never be stated unambiguously, as a means of reflection it surpasses all systems made up of concepts with fixed definitions. The fact that such systems nevertheless exert a powerful attraction upon many people derives, for Tomberg, not least from the fact that they expect such systems to increase the extent of their own power. Closed systems of thought seem to make it easier to orient ourselves; they allow any uncertainty to be set aside by a pre-established framework, without any appreciable effort on our own part.

The creators of systems simplify complex realities by taking "*one* thing as known or given, and, by reducing multiplicity (that is, many other things) to this one thing, propose to explain it with its help." (112) In this way, they keep solutions that seem compelling for logical thought close at hand for any problem:

> For Marxists, it is child's play to answer any question whatever. This is because they have ready to hand a mechanical apparatus, a *system*, that takes on the greater part of the labor of answering questions. *The system does the work for them.* Systems are so attractive and fascinating because they do most of the thinking for people—thereby increasing, not their skill, but their power. (110)

Tomberg, whose own mother had been murdered in the confusion after the October Revolution, and who himself fled from the Soviet sphere of power, wrote these lines in the political atmosphere of the Cold War. His critique was by no means directed only at Marxism, however, but against *all* systems that tended to absolutism, that wished to "reduce multiplicity to this *one* thing" that stands in the center of their thought.

Whether we think of Marxism (which regards every form of human culture as a superstructural phenomenon of the economic base) or of psychoanalysis (which explains them as sublimated libido), from Tomberg's perspective both systems behave like the totalitarian Church theology of the late Middle Ages, which attempted

> to elaborate a comprehensive, ironclad "system" with which to bring people's minds and hearts and ways of life under its control. (147)

Every system of this kind

> is in principle filled with the spirit of the Inquisition and in practice (whenever circumstances allow) creates an "inquisitional machinery." (147)

Wherever, by contrast, there is the belief that God and the world are not to be explained and supposedly understood by means of constraining systems, but instead to be intimated by means of a symbol approaching ever closer to an understanding never fully achieved, one can remain open, learning, and patient. Because his work on personal certainty necessarily entailed long passages of philosophical argument, Tomberg clearly felt the need to supplement these passages increasingly with intensive forays into symbolism. He wished to devote the sixth chapter, which was broken off after a short introduction, to the Kabbalistic symbols of the ten names of God.[7] He had previously emphasized, at the end of the fifth chapter, that symbols served the ends of "*personal* deepening" without any "claim to scientificity." Indeed, this unfinished, open work ends on the note of a renunciation of objectively verifiable truth.

---

[7] Tomberg returned to this theme in considerable detail in his last major work, *Proclamation on Sinai: Covenant and Commandments.*

The Value of, and the
Problems Connected with, the Fragment

Anyone who is interested in Tomberg's work can recognize many aspects of his later writings in the present text. Thus, the ideas on sleeping and waking consciousness are later developed in *Lazarus: The Miracle of Resurrection in World History*. Similar remarks on symbolism as the appropriate medium for the expression of inner experiences are formulated in his *Meditations on the Tarot: A Journey into Christian Hermeticism*. Many ideas can now be traced back to the context in which they originated, because this fragment offers us a glimpse of an early phase in the development of these and other motifs. At the same time, many statements are expressed more succinctly here than in the sometimes more intricate contents of the later books.

A fragment of text left behind by its author and never prepared for publication by him naturally presents formal and material difficulties. One such difficulty concerns the way sources are dealt with. If Tomberg provides precise references for citations from works such as those of the biologist Edgar Dacqué and the logician Rudolf Carnap, in other places such information is lacking. This is particularly true in the case of Tomberg's use of classic literature. Thus, the typescript begins with a legend whose source is given by Tomberg as the *Book of the Penitence of Adam (Paenitentiae Adae Liber)*. By this he may have meant the apocryphal and prohibited *Liber Paenitentiae Adae*, named in the *Decretum Gelasianum de libris recipiendis et non recipiendis*, which is perhaps identical with the *Vita Adae et Evae*, or the *Apocalypse of Moses*. It remains unclear, however, which of the extant versions of the *Vita Adae et Evae* Tomberg used. Moreover, he evidently associated motifs from this Late-

Antique text with Christian traditions about the discovery of the true cross such as those retold by Jacobus de Voragine in the *Golden Legend* and by other sources, which he, however, similarly ascribed to the *Liber Paenitentiae Adae*.[8] References for the provenance of statements on ideas taken from Chinese and Indian philosophy, as well as other themes, were also absent from the fragment.[9] Likewise, some of Tomberg's brief characterizations, for instance of Islam, Sufism, and shamans, would benefit from more documentation (which perhaps Tomberg had intended to provide). Further critical annotations would be useful as well regarding his interpretations of Immanuel Kant's philosophy and the examples he introduces from science. But in the end, such considerations are irrelevant to an understanding of the text's fundamental reflections.

We will perhaps best do justice to the attempt at a total or holistic method that was begun in this manuscript, and then foundered in it, by enjoying the text principally as an invitation to meditation, or as a work of art and spiritual opening, over and above all the philosophical ideas contained in it. Those who study the several works Tomberg composed *after* he abandoned this present text may well find themselves returning to it ever and again as a spring of fresh, living water that flowed onward through other channels while gathering strength over the course of his further life and writings.

[8] See footnote on page 1 of the present text.
[9] Some of these have been located and provided in this edition.

Preface

Ask, and it shall be given you;
seek, and ye shall find;
knock, and it shall be opened unto you.
    —The Master

HE *Book of the Penitence of Adam*[1] TELLS HOW Adam's third son, Seth, became his heir and successor. Since he was just, it was permitted him to reach the gate of the Earthly Paradise. Thus he saw the Tree of Knowledge and the Tree of Life, which grew in such an entwined fashion that they formed a single Tree. And with the permission of the All-Highest, the cherub to whom the Ancient of Days had entrusted the guardianship of the gates of Eden gave Seth three seeds, which contained the powers and the essence of that Tree.

The *Book of the Penitence of Adam* further relates that

---

[1] After mentioning this title in his typescript, Tomberg adds in parentheses the words *Poenitentiae Adae Liber*. As it happens, the Gelasian Decree (regarding the "received" biblical canon) does mention a "Liber qui appellatur Paenitentia Adae," but the *Jewish* text to which this reference most likely refers cannot be the source of the *Christian* legend Tomberg refers to. The *Book of the Penitence of Adam* he speaks of appears to be a manuscript dealing with kabbalistic traditions kept in the Bibliothèque de l'Arsenal in Paris. It recounts the legend, current in the Middle Ages, that the Cross of the Crucifixion was, ultimately, made from the Trees of Knowledge and of Life. This complex of medieval tales, with many variants, is known more generally as the "Legend of the Rood."

1

when Adam died, Seth, following the cherub's instructions, placed in his father's mouth the three seeds—the three seeds of life without end. The shoots that grew from these seeds became the bush that burned without being consumed, from the midst of which the All-Highest revealed to Moses His eternal Name: I AM THE I AM. Moses took from that sacred bush a three-branched bough which he made his wonder-working staff. Although separated from its rootstock, that bough lived on and blossomed again and was later preserved in the Ark of the Covenant.

The *Book of the Penitence of Adam* further relates that King David planted that same three-branched bough upon Mount Zion, whence Solomon his son later took wood from what was now grown a triple or three-trunked tree to construct the twin pillars of Jachin and Boaz at the entrance to the Temple in Jerusalem. The insides of these pillars were of wood of two of the trunks, and their outsides clad in bronze. Another portion of wood, from the third trunk, was set into the threshold of the great gate of the Temple, so that no unclean thing might enter the sanctuary.

The *Book of the Penitence of Adam* further relates that certain malicious Levite priests one night removed this impediment to their unholy designs, weighted it with stone, and threw it into the Temple reservoir, where it sank. Since that time, an angel of the All-Highest has stirred the waters of the pool so that water from below should rise to the top and water from the top should sink below. In this way, the water of the pool became miraculously purifying and healing—on which account the people were diverted from seeking out in its depths the tree of Solomon.

The *Book of the Penitence of Adam* further relates that when, in the days of Jesus Christ, the pool was drained to be cleansed, the Jews discovered the submerged beam. Thinking it worthless, they took it out of Jerusalem and threw it across the brook Kedron. And it came to pass that after our Redeemer was arrested by night in the garden of Gethsemane, he had to pass over this very beam; and when he did, his executioners pushed him from it into the water below. Then, in their haste to prepare the main instrument of his passion, they took with them the beam comprised of three woods, from which they fashioned the cross upon which he was crucified.

The present work grew out of the same substance from which this legend grew.

Introduction

Dass ich erkenne, was die Welt
Im Innersten zusammenhält
Schau' alle Wirkenskraft und Samen—
Und tu' nicht mehr in Worten kramen
—*Faust*

So that I should know what the world
contains in its most inward parts,
behold the efficacious seeds of all power,
and no longer rummage about in words.

HE PRESENT WORK[1] TAKES FOR ITS SUBJECT LIFE as it is revealed spiritually, psychologically, and biologically. It is about humanity's path toward truth, i.e., toward life in truth, or true life.

The subject is as large as the world is. Consequently, we will make use here of the "total method." The method on which the work is based is the total exertion of the total human being in order to arrive at a total result. Hence it embraces lived experience, observation, study, conscience, thinking, feeling, guided imagination, intimations, prayers, immersion, and more. Its results represent the *harmony* of the individual results achieved in various ways and by

---

[1] At the outset, Tomberg described this book as his life-work. He was, however, destined to leave it unfinished and move on to his masterwork, *Meditations on the Tarot: A Journey into Christian Hermeticism*, among other important later works.

means of various human capacities. Thus, that which corresponds (for example) to the sense of logic, the sense of value, the moral sense, the sense of beauty, and the sense of health, is described as "true," and regarded as a "result."

Whom should the author thank for help, stimulation, direction, and instruction? Who are the author's *teachers*? The author is indebted to innumerable people for instruction and stimulation. They shine like stars in the firmament of his consciousness. But they are also as numerous as the stars in the night sky. The author's sky has also, however, its moon, which makes the nocturnal—or deeper—side of his life visible in the silver magic of its light. And also a sun, to which he owes the brightness and warmth of day. *What* the author owes to them, and *who* they are, will become so obvious, clear, and self-evident in reading the book that there is no need to name names at this point.

What is described here as a "total method" will indeed later (if any attention at all is paid to the book) be described by some commentators as "existentialism," by others as "syncretism" or "eclecticism," by still others as "anti-specialism," and so on. It certainly is all these things, but it is one thing more: it is a traversing of all the paths that may be walked by human beings without endangering their spiritual and bodily health. It is therefore no accident if in this book the reader should, on the one hand, meet such thinkers as Kant, Fichte, Schelling, Solovyov, Berdyaev, and Russell, and on the other the creators of works of Kabbalah, of Yoga, of Christian and Chinese mysticism—for they are all of them *human beings*, and all strove as *human beings* for *human* knowledge of life.

How indeed can anyone be justified in asserting that the efforts and results of only *one* among them, or of only *one* particular group among them, are of value, while all others do not even merit an honest engagement with them? Who can be justified in saying that there are people who, for all their efforts, have not achieved anything essential, even if they themselves assert the opposite?

The total method means not only a total exertion of the whole being of an individual person, but also paying attention to and putting to use the exertions of the whole of humanity in the course of world history insofar as it is accessible to us.

I

A Meditation
on Sleeping and Waking

Could ye not watch with me one hour?
—*The Master*, in Gethsemane

F SLEEPING AND WAKING WERE TWO STATES sharply separated in time, and mutually exclusive, so that we ought to say that a person is either sleeping or waking (if, that is, it were really only a case of "either/or"), then we would neither have the ability to wake up at the right time without an alarm clock nor ever be "absent-minded" when awake. We would never forget something, or fail to attend to something of importance to us, by "oversleeping." Sleeping and waking reach into each other: there is a light, "waking" sleep; there is also a sluggish, "sleepy" waking. Sleep accompanies us during our waking; waking accompanies our sleep and influences it, just as sleep plays into our waking state. While awake, we are awake only in part: in many respects, we sleep on.

While asleep, moreover, we are so only in part: in many respects we are, even while asleep, still awake. Even in sleep, we remain awake to certain sense impressions: we actively react to them. This holds true not only for impressions of touch and hearing, but even of sight: the sudden appearance of a bright light awakens many people. "Awakens"

them: meaning, they actively react to these impressions; they do not "oversleep" them, but are "awake" to them.

On the other hand, there are many things to which we are asleep while yet waking. Thus there are people who, for example, are asleep to questions about their worldview or to world events or to religion. Then one day it can happen that they wake up to these things. Still others are asleep to certain moral duties and tasks in their lives. All of us have had the experience of waking up—not only of waking up in the morning to the outside world in general, but also of waking up to particular things in our so-called waking life. Everyone has this experience during the period of transition from childhood to adolescence. To how many things we were asleep during childhood, things that later became so significant and indispensable!

Maturing is really the process of a series of experiences of waking up, one after another. To be mature is to be awake to the essential concerns of human life. The wider the extent of the things to which we are awake, and the more deeply we are awake to these things, the more mature we are. Indeed, waking up also has its *inner* degrees in relation to a given thing: quite apart from the magnitude of the span over which our waking up extends, it also has degrees of intensity. We can be only quite superficially awake to many things; we can also, however, be awake to only a few things, but awake to them with great intensity.

That sleeping and waking have many degrees and can be of different kinds, that they reach into each other and at the same time represent strata that are actually present in us, is not only known to the modern depth psychology of each of its three main schools (those of Freud, Adler, and Jung), but also forms the basis for such world-famous spiri-

10

tual and religious practical methods as those of Buddhism, Yoga, and the *Spiritual Exercises* (*Exercitia spiritualia*) of St Ignatius of Loyola.

Buddhism. The practice of Buddhism rests on the experience of awakening to particular things to which we had been asleep. Prince Gautama became a Buddha ("Buddha" meaning "one who is awakened") by awakening under the bodhi tree to the "four noble truths." He awoke to the aspect of suffering in life: he suddenly knew, in a quite different way, what he had long "known." Every adult person knows well enough—as did Gautama also, after he had left the royal palace and gone on his travels—that birth, sickness, ageing, and death are afflictions, and that to be joined to non-love and to be separated from love are afflictions also. But "enlightenment" beneath the bodhi tree means something more: a knowledge of what one already knew, an understanding of what was already understood, in a new way.

An insight comes about under the bodhi tree that far outstrips in brightness and wakefulness any "mere head-knowledge" experienced in a state of half-sleep. With his thoughts, his feelings, and his will, the Prince understood how wide was the scope, and how extensive the effects, of suffering in human life. He *awoke* to suffering in human life—to the same suffering that had long been "known" to him. This awakening also contained (or naturally brought with it) an insight into the original cause of suffering, of the annihilation of this original cause, and of the path that leads to this annihilation. That is, the indivisible organism of the "four noble truths" dawned on him as degrees of awakening to suffering. He understood with his whole being what he had until then understood with a part only.

And this is the very nature of awakening: insight—i.e., understanding, truly feeling, and truly willing "into" the whole human being. That is, total knowledge.

The practice of Buddhism consists in putting to use the experience of awakening—doing so by striving to exercise it systematically. In this exercise it is, in particular, a question of understanding more deeply what is already understood, i.e., of bringing what is "already understood" to the complete comprehension of our total human nature. For this reason, it is a matter of repeated *immersion* in particular formulas and ideas with the intention and the hope (perhaps after a thousandfold repetition) of awakening to the realities expressed or designated by these formulas and ideas. That these exertions are occasionally crowned with success is sufficiently evident from the fact that the Buddhist practice of immersion is still alive and well today. It cannot be believed that a practice of this kind could have kept itself going for almost two-and-a-half-thousand years if it had always been unsuccessful!

Indian Yoga. We are familiar also with the practice of Indian Yoga, with its repeated immersion in particular formulas and ideas. Formulas such as *tat tvam asi* ("thou art that") or *aham brahmasmi* ("I am Brahma") contain *in themselves* a whole scale of immersion—that is, of a gradual awakening to their content. In a different and much later connection, Kant contrasted the "transcendental subject" ("the thinker in thinking and the seer in seeing," as it is put in the language of the Upanishads) with the "empirical subject" (*ahamkara*: the "I-illusion"). Fichte described this "I" as the only reality within the world of our experience. And Hegel proclaimed the identity of this "I" with the

World Spirit. For the Kantians, Fichteans, and Hegelians, that settled the matter.

Not so, however, in ancient India. There the doctrine of the identity of the transcendental self (*atman*) with the divinity of the world (*brahman*) became the practice of bringing this doctrine about *in reality*; that is, it became Yoga. Here, it was and still is a matter not merely of holding this identity to be true, but also of awakening fully to it. The degrees of immersion in Yoga—commencing with simple concentration (*dharana*), passing through the stage of contemplation (*dhyana*) to the stage where consciousness as a whole becomes one with the object of immersion (*samadhi*)—begin just where most philosophy leaves off.

Philosophers (at least in the West) come to a halt once they have arrived at a conceptually clear, logically or experientially well-grounded and clearly-defined view. Their concern as philosophers is thereby at an end: as far as they are concerned, they have clearly and convincingly accounted for how matters stand and why they cannot be otherwise. For practitioners of Yoga, however, this end-result of philosophical thinking only marks the beginning of what *they* are concerned with. For them, this result of philosophical observation signifies an opening to immerse themselves in it: to think, feel, will, breathe, and live themselves further into the object until they are completely *awakened* to it.

Spiritual Exercises of St Ignatius of Loyola. A further example of the practical application of the insight that human beings are partly asleep even when awake, and that they are always capable of awakening further, is provided by the *Spiritual Exercises* of St Ignatius of Loyola, founder of the Jesuit order. These exercises date from more than four hundred years ago. Pope Paul III recommended them in 1548 in his papal brief *Pastoralis officii cura* as "full of piety and holiness, most useful and curative for the strengthening and spiritual progress of the faithful." In his encyclical *Mens nostra* of December 20, 1929,[1] Pope Pius XI speaks of St Ignatius of Loyola as the all-surpassing, true master of all spiritual exercises. These two papal writings show that St Ignatius's *Spiritual Exercises* were no less prized in the twentieth century than they were in the sixteenth. The reason for this lies in the fact that today, as four centuries ago, they awaken those who practice them to particular concerns. They render them awake to a quite different aspect of life than does, for example, the spiritual practice of awakening in Buddhism. In Buddhism, it is a question of awakening to the aspect of *suffering* in life. In the spiritual exercises of St Ignatius it is a matter of awakening the will to cooperate in the work of *healing the suffering* in life. This will is awakened by contrasting the empire of sin with the kingdom of salvation in its full intensity and concrete actuality.

---

[1] In this encyclical, Pope Pius XI writes, concerning Ignatius of Loyola's spiritual exercises: "And in very deed, the excellence of spiritual doctrine altogether free from the perils and errors of false mysticism, the admirable facility of adapting the exercises to any order or state of man, whether they devote themselves to contemplation in the cloisters, or lead an active life in the affairs of the world, the apt coordination of the various parts, the wonderful and lucid order in the meditation of truths that seem to follow naturally one from another; and lastly the spiritual lessons which after casting off the yoke of sin and washing away the diseases inherent in his morals lead a man through the safe paths of abnegation and the removal of evil habits up to the supreme heights of prayer and divine love; without doubt all these are things which sufficiently show the efficacious nature of the Ignatian method and abundantly commend the Ignatian meditations."

Over the course of the four weeks of the exercises, those putting them into practice become conscious of the nature and extent of sin both in themselves and in humanity as a whole. They arrive at a concrete insight into and appreciation of the ultimate consequences of sin. Then they become conscious of the meaning and scope of the salvation placed before their spiritual gaze by the birth, miraculous healings, sufferings, death, and resurrection of Jesus Christ. In consequence, there awakens in them the will to make an uncompromising choice, the will to make a choice that is one hundred per cent honest in the face of their conscience and knowledge. After this, they contemplate step by step the irresistible beauty of love become flesh, its true nobility (the only true nobility there is); the freedom of breathing in love (the only true freedom there is); its depth, which makes everything else appear shallow in comparison with it; the fullness of life that streams out of it (the only true life there is)—and everything else in it, everything that is so true, so original, so living, so creative and unmechanical… The practitioners finish the exercises with burning hearts: they now have complete certainty that God is love and that whoever lives in love lives in God, and God in him; that love is stronger than death and that Christ is resurrected and lives and is calling them and all others to participate in His life. The prayer of one of the first practitioners of the exercises, a direct pupil of St Ignatius, comes from a heart set afire by them:

> I love You and will always love You, not so that You make me blest in Heaven, not so as to escape eternal damnation, not in the hope of any sort of reward, but as You have loved me, only because You are my King. Amen.

This prayer by St Francis Xavier expresses the fruit of the spiritual exercises in the clearest possible way: in it, the heart awakened to love speaks the authentic and pure language of the heart. For the human heart, when it is awakened, and when it is permitted to speak in its own language, knows no weighing up of advantage and disadvantage, in time or eternity. Nothing of the salesman, of the wage-laborer, or of the person insisting upon his rights, survives within it.

In St Francis Xavier we have an illustration of the state of consciousness that is the realization of the third stage of the spiritual exercises, the stage of the "path to unification," which is preceded by the stages of the "path of illumination" and the "path of purification." In the four "weeks" of the complete spiritual exercises of St Ignatius, awakening to the realities of sin and salvation is the "path of purification"; awakening to the value of the salvation offered to us is the "path of illumination"; and the burning up of the heart in love is the stage of the "path of unification."

The thirty days of the spiritual exercises represent the time of a total effort to awaken to the reality of love as the highest value and the true vocation of humanity. Those who work through the exercises in a serious way and with unreserved honesty become "witnesses" to the reality and value of love. They obtain personal certainty about it from a personal experience that no one and nothing can take away from them. They can certainly be killed, but no one can take their experience away from them. They have breathed a new kind of air and have known its ozone. Henceforth, no other kind of air will ever be able to replace this for them.

Immanuel Kant. Numerous examples of the awakening of the sleeping or slumbering layers of consciousness are afforded also by the history of philosophy and science. When Kant, for instance, looking back on his intellectual life, speaks of having "awakened from his dogmatic slumbers" (an awakening to which he owes his transcendental method and his critical scrutiny of the whole field of philosophical and scientific knowledge), it is a case of a layer of consciousness becoming active—one that had previously been passively immersed in slumber. The awakening Kant means is the insight that we can think not only about the objects of experience, but also about thinking itself. This is the awakening whose consequences he himself found so significant that he could compare it only to the "discovery made by Copernicus."

What had taken place in Kant was a "repositioning" of consciousness from identifying itself with the process of thinking to observing and evaluating that very process. The "dogmatic slumber" that preceded this repositioning consisted in Kant having naively surrendered his consciousness to thinking: hitherto, his consciousness had been carried along with the current of thinking and become one with it. Now, however, his consciousness picked itself up so as to free itself—lifted itself up as it were from this current in order to observe it from a vantage point above the process of thinking—and by so doing was enabled to determine its direction and limits instead of being carried along by it.

This act of consciousness tearing itself free from the current of thought and discovering a higher vantage point (from which the activity of thinking could be observed, inspected, judged, and guided) is the achievement of a consciousness impelled by an extraordinary honesty and love for the truth such as indeed deserves to be compared with the "discovery made by Copernicus." For many of the presumptuous claims of rationalism had to be given up as a result of Kant's *Critique of Pure Reason*. His three "critiques" (of pure reason, of the power of judgment, and of practical reason) opened the way to a much more serious and adequate knowledge—to the knowledge that results from the *connection* between insights won in three different ways, by means of three different human capacities.

Philosophy has Kant to thank, however, not only for having rebuked reason for its claim to sole validity, not only for his emphasis on the value of the two other capacities of human consciousness (the power of judgment, and practical reason), but also for a new experience that the transcendental method (the inner observation of the process of thinking from a higher vantage point) brings with it. This experience is that of the reality of the transcendental self, which is higher than the empirical self. For when I make my thinking the object of intuition, I become conscious of myself as an observer of thinking. This higher vantage point from which the process of thought can be inspected means, at the same time, experiencing the self, which is just as independent of the process of thought as that same self is independently experienced *by* the process of thought. From this, moreover, results the certainty of *freedom*, that is, the reality of morality as the capacity to bring about *new* causes within the realm of determined causal sequence (the chain of causes and effects in nature). This is what acting freely and morally means.

Kant's doctrine that only the unforced actions that proceed from and are performed by persons ("moral autonomy") are of ethical value—and that persons are in fact capable of such free (i.e., ethical) actions—rests, not on pragmatic, utilitarian, or rationalistic grounds, but on the *experience* of the self that is higher than the empirical subject and is consequently independent of the empirical subject, and thus *free*.

This brings us to the reason for Kant's insistence on the *concept of duty* as the highest concept of ethics. Kant wanted to place a concept of this kind in the foreground of ethics—a concept that expresses in the clearest and purest way possible the difference between the empirical subject and the transcendental subject—in order to *intensify* this difference until it appears to be an *opposition*. It was in the concept of duty that an opposition most clearly appeared for Kant between the empirical self with its inclinations and disinclinations, its wishes and hopes, on the one hand, and the pure *ought* of the transcendental self on the other, an ought that can be opposed to inclinations, wishes, and hopes of any kind.

Love, loyalty, courage, and so on, are unfitted to express this opposition because they can appear in a way that is mingled with inclinations, wishes, and hopes; indeed, they can be confused with the latter. Those who act out of love also have their inclinations and wishes present in the action. And who can say with certainty that their action does not spring from this inclination and these wishes? For Kant, then, there is only certainty about the source of an action if this action, while it is unforced and free, tends in the *opposite* direction from the inclinations and wishes of the person acting. And there is such certainty as this only in actions performed out of *duty*, since only in acting out of duty do we find, in its sharpest form, the opposition between inclination and moral consciousness, between wishing-for and ought, between the empirical subject and the transcendental subject.

19

The concept of duty made it possible for Kant to point to an opposition between the transcendental self and the empirical self in the moral realm, an opposition just as clear and susceptible of being experienced and lived-out as the same opposition had been shown to be in the realm of cognition by Kant's transcendental method. But Kant was unable to conceive of duty as an ultimate,[2] for it was he who had postulated immortality from the fact of the human being's striving for infinite perfectibility. If, for Kant, the immortality of the individual consciousness necessarily follows from the striving for a perfection that is infinitely to be realized, how could he posit his current concept of duty as something ultimate and finally valid for all eternity?

Freedom, which shows itself most clearly in an action performed out of the pure consciousness of duty, has in view as many further stages of its perfecting as are made possible by the eternity of the immortality that is necessary precisely for this end. That which *today* (at today's stage) commands obedience from my inclinations and wishes as a strict duty, may *tomorrow* (at a higher stage) have obtained the voluntary assent of my inclinations and wishes, and may *the day after tomorrow* (at a yet higher stage) comprehend my total being, including *all* its inclinations and wishes, in a burning unity. Put another way: that which is "duty" today, can be "beauty" tomorrow; and the day after tomorrow, it can become that concord of "willing and the ought"[3] which can be described as "love."

---

[2] *Als Letztes,* considered as a technical term in Kant's transcendental method, may perhaps be rendered "as a transcendental," but this would require more discussion, and need not detain the reader here.

[3] *Wollen und Sollen.*

Kant was a long way from denying the subsequent development of the consciousness of beauty from the concept of duty; what he intended, rather, was the denial of those feelings and moods that are inclined to describe themselves as "love" but are not mature enough to meet the strict demands of duty. True moral life in Kant's sense *begins* with duty; once it *has* thus begun, however, there is no end to the process of its further perfecting. There is a morality "before duty" and a morality "after duty"; the first is relative and finite, the latter absolute and infinite, even with respect to the number of its stages.

The awakening from "dogmatic slumber," and its consequences in Kant's life, are not to be seen as a new kind of dogmatic slumber. "Duty" in Kant's sense is not the terminus of the human path, but its beginning—indispensable to all. It is the beginning of this path because it signifies *the experience of the reality of freedom*. It thereby also signifies the beginning of ethical life as such. For ethical life and freedom are one. Only ethical consciousness is truly human, since of earth's creatures only human beings are capable of freedom. Everything unfree, by contrast, is unethical and subhuman.

Only the free person is truly a person, and all unfreedom is subhuman. An awakening to this aspect of human nobility took place and shone out once upon a time in Königsberg, the city of Kant. The light of this awakening to the nobility of the human being and of the human vocation has, since then, shone out to many people right across the world. Kant's home city of Königsberg, however, the city whence the freedom of human individuality was proclaimed with a sound sobriety that has never been bettered, has since become Kaliningrad, so named to honor the collectivism to which the Russian worker Kalinin[4] was devoted. Here we face a great and tragic symbol of the spiritual history of humanity: Königsberg has become Kaliningrad.

⊕

Symbolism. When I say "we face a great and tragic symbol of the spiritual history of humanity: Königsberg has become Kaliningrad," much is meant that goes beyond the initial formulation. What is *intimated* by the sentence exceeds its immediate propositional content. The sentence is a *symbol,* and is meant for symbolic use: not to compel or persuade anyone towards an insight, but to *stimulate* them. And here we are furnished with a further illustrative example of awakening from a waking sleep. For symbolism, symbolic language *as such* is that kind of language which reckons with the fact of the many levels of wakefulness and the continual presence of sleep in human consciousness, and aims at demonstrating this—aims, that is, at *awakening* human consciousness. The language of symbolism, which is as old as the full reach of the spiritual history of humanity (so far as we can know that history), is and was always applied where it was a matter of addressing people from beyond the level at which their consciousness is, or was, currently awake.

The sign-language of mathematics or logic, however (including modern so-called "symbolic logic"), is *not* a sym-

---

[4] Mikhail Ivanovich Kalinin (1875–1946) labored as a metal worker in St. Petersburg, took part in the 1905 Russian Revolution, and was an early member of the Bolsheviks. He served as head of state of the Russian Federative Socialist Republic and later the Soviet Union from 1919 to 1946. From 1926, he was a member of the Politburo of the Communist Party of the Soviet Union.

bolic language. This is because it owes its existence precisely to the attempt completely to *exclude* the symbolic element that is always contained in ordinary languages, and to put signs in the place of this symbolic element, signs that are to be (as far as possible) free of any material content—i.e., that are to represent an abstraction taken to the furthest possible degree. A symbol is not an abstraction. It is an emblem[5] (*Sinnbild*), i.e., an image (*Bild*) filled with meaning or sense (*Sinn*) residing in the dimension of *depth*. In order to grasp this deeper meaning or sense, layers of consciousness must be activated that until then had reposed behind the layer of ordinary waking consciousness.

When, for example, we consider the first two of the three principles of traditional Aristotelian logic (the principle of identity and the principle of non-contradiction[6])—expressed by the formulas "A equals A" and "A cannot both be B and not be B"—what we find in these formulas is not a symbolism. It is, rather, a minimum of imagery, pure abstraction, that comes as close as can be to the ideal of *formal* monovalence and *material* polyvalence or indifference. If we expand these propositions to include the third principle (that of the excluded middle), we see that they imply: "Everything is what it is" (principle of identity), "a thing cannot be thus and thus and *not* be thus and thus" (principle of non-contradiction), and "a thing is either thus and thus or it is not thus and thus" (principle of the excluded middle). Here, "thing" can mean a cow, a person, a number, a concept, or anything else we like.

---

[5] *Bild*: "image/picture"; *Sinn*: "sense/meaning"; *Sinnbild*: "imaged meaning/emblem," or in a more general sense, simply "symbol."

[6] The third being the principle of the excluded middle.

If we now compare the content and form of the three traditional principles of logic (in modern logic they have been supplemented by a number of further propositions) with the Preface of the Most Holy Trinity that forms a part of the usual Sunday mass, we can arrive at a living intuition of the difference between the conceptual language of a statically conceived waking consciousness and the symbolic language of a dynamically conceived waking-sleeping consciousness.

The Preface reads:

> *Vere dignum et iustum est, aequum et salutare, nos tibi semper et ubique gratias agere: Domine sancte, Pater omnipotens, aeterne Deus: Qui cum unigenito Filio tuo et Spiritu Sancto unus es Deus, unus es Dominus: non in unius singularitate personae, sed in unius Trinitate substantiae.*

> It is truly right and just, our duty and our salvation, always and everywhere to give you thanks, Lord, holy Father, almighty and eternal God. For with your Only Begotten Son and the Holy Spirit you are one God, one Lord: not in the unity of a single person, but in a Trinity of one substance.

This text speaks in symbolic language, i.e., it is directed to the presently waking consciousness—but exceeds it. This is because, although it does contain two of the three principles of logic—the principle of identity ("eternal God") and that of the excluded middle ("*one* God, *one* Lord")—it also exceeds them by saying that the Father, Son, and Holy Spirit are different persons, who, however, are *one* God in *one* essential being.

In other words, if we do not rise to an essentially new level of consciousness, or awaken within us a new level of consciousness to activity, but try instead to approach the text with the means of waking consciousness alone (i.e., solely with the three principles of logic), we will find that the principles of logic both hold and do not hold here, which is to say that they have been exceeded. The principle of identity is exceeded in that it is said that the Father is both himself *and* at the same time is identical with the Son and the Holy Spirit. The principle of non-contradiction is exceeded in that it is said that unity and triplicity are set out as one. And the principle of the excluded middle is exceeded also in that it is said that the person of the Father actually *is* and yet also *is not*, since it is identical with the essential Being of the other two persons of the Trinity.

There is here an unmistakable call to awaken to a higher activity of consciousness—to awaken from the "logic of the thing" to the "logic of love." Those who have loved, and who have been loved, know from experience that in love the miracle of unity and difference takes place; they know that in love the Thou is as real as the I, and that the I does not thereby disappear.

This experience supplies ideas and thoughts of a kind that make it possible (by means of the way of analogy) for consciousness to worship the Most Holy Trinity addressed in the Preface in a way that is *really* prayerful—that is, not to face it in a way that is alien and devoid of understanding, but to kneel worshipfully before the truly divine cosmic miracle of love. And this kneeling will then be the expression of the awakening of a layer of consciousness that until then was asleep.

There are many examples in all areas of human life of the mobility of the frontiers of waking consciousness and of the practice of awakening the sleeping layers of consciousness.

In the examples given here it was only a matter of showing that waking consciousness is not a constant quantity, and that there were and are practical methods of expanding the frontiers of consciousness.

⊕

Intoxication and Frenzy. In connection with the question of the waking and sleeping states of consciousness, one further state of consciousness must be considered, a state that belongs neither to a true waking state nor to a real state of sleep: the state of *intoxication* and *frenzy*. The overstepping of the principles of logic, as illustrated with the example of the Preface of the Most Holy Trinity, is opposed to the drunken or frenzied state of consciousness in which logic is not exceeded but cast away. In this sense, the Preface of the Most Holy Trinity may be contrasted with the text of the "magic square" in Goethe's *Faust*:

Du musst verstehn!	You must understand!
Aus Eins mach' Zehn,	Out of one I make ten,
Und Zwei lass' gehn.	And let two go.
Und Drei mach' gleich,	Make three even,
So bist du reich.	And you will be rich.
Verlier die Vier!	Lose the four!
Aus Fünf und Sechs,	Out of five and six,
So sagt die Hex',	So says the witch,
Mach' Sieben und Acht,	I make seven and eight,
So ist's vollbracht:	And then it's done:
Und Neun ist Eins,	And nine is one,
Und Zehn ist keins.	And ten is none.
Das ist das Hexeneinmaleins!	Thus the witches' magic square!

The witch adds this commentary:

Die hohe Kraft	The great strength
Der Wissenschaft,	Of science
Der ganzen Welt verborgen!	Has hidden the entire world!
Und wer nicht denkt,	And whoever does not think,
Dem wird sie geschenkt,	To him the world is gifted:
Er hat sie ohne Sorgen.	He has it without even trying.

"And whoever does not think, to him the world is gifted" is the "epistemology" not only of witches, but also of sects of "enthusiasts" such as, for example, that of the *khlysty* in Russia (described in Russian author Melnikov-Petschersky's *In the Forests* and *On the Hills*),[7] or the whirling dervishes of the Islamic East, the shamans of Siberia, and the sorcerers of the peoples of Africa. This "epistemology" is found, however, not only among the simple folk of the people or among primitives: "holy intoxication," orgies, and "sacred madness" are honored as well among highly civilized peoples and cultural classes.

The state of intoxication by means of which people manage to do away with thinking can easily be mistaken, however, for the awakening and the wakefulness of higher levels of consciousness. The excitement and intensity of the state of intoxication can easily be interpreted as an elevated activity of consciousness. But here it is not a case of awakening, or of sleep. It is an invasion on the part of the sleepwalking *dream consciousness*, which is neither waking nor sleeping,

---

[7] Pavel Ivanovich Melnikov (1818–1883) published under the name Andrei Pechersky the two novels Tomberg mentions (*In den Wäldern* and *Auf den Bergen*) in 1875 and 1881 respectively. The *khlysty* were an ecstatic and ascetic religious sect that arose in seventeenth-century Russia.

but represents instead a chaotic mixture of the two states. Since the regulating efficacy of thinking and conscience has been shut down, it is disordered and thus a mixture of the different layers of consciousness: the higher and the lower, the human and the subhuman.

The *true* awakening of new layers of consciousness has nothing in common with the state of intoxication, drunkenness, and frenzy. The "enthusiasm" that accompanies such true awakening, and that constitutes its inner potency, is that of *intensifying calm*, of an inner stillness that grows ever more still. Any who have even only once experienced the starry heaven on a bright silver moonlit night will understand what is meant here by the enthusiasm of intensifying calm, by the enthusiasm of an *inner* stillness that becomes ever more still. They will understand that calm is not merely an absence of excitement; it is, rather, a growing strength of consciousness that increases in clarity, collectedness, and firmness. Calmness is strength of spirit; it is the state in which true waking and true sleep are joined and shake hands; it is the state in which waking and sleep, waking and sleeping layers of consciousness, *resonate* with each other.

⊕

Sleeplessness. This brings us to consider a further aspect of the question of sleeping and waking: that of sleeplessness. For it can happen that when we bring sleeping layers of consciousness to ever greater wakefulness, we become *hyperawake*—that is, sleepless. Sleepiness and sleeplessness are twin ailments that can be experienced not only in the physical realm but also in that of the life of consciousness. Our consciousness is sleepy when a state of disinterestedness comes into play. Our consciousness is sleepless when waking consciousness seems to tear itself free of the resting layers of deep consciousness and emancipate itself from them, so that it is not only awake, but also slams shut all doors that connect it to these deeper layers.

This happens when, for example, we become *fanatical*: when we close ourselves off from things that contradict the system of principles and moral rules we have built for ourselves. Waking consciousness is always cut off from deep consciousness when we lose our joy in learning, in modifying our ideas, and experience instead a disinclination to move beyond a circle of fixed, ready-made institutions, or to allow anything new and unexpected to enter into this circle. Fanatics (those who have become incapable of changing their ideas) can neither wake up nor properly sleep. For proper waking up is learning; and proper sleep is growth. Waking means experience; but sleep means transformation. Experience is *acquired* in waking consciousness; growth and change of nature *happen* in sleep. This is true both of the body and of consciousness.

The building-up or anabolic activity of the organism predominates in the state of sleep but grows *fatigued* in waking consciousness as a result of breaking-down or catabolic activity. So also, becoming, or spiritual growth, happens (for it cannot be *made*) in the deep layers of consciousness, whereas bright, waking consciousness is predominantly an outlay that leads to a spent, exhausted consciousness. We meet people exhausted in their consciousness as often as we do physically fatigued, sleep-deprived people. It is indeed rare to meet an important scientist whose monotonous and unresonant speech, toneless voice, and dead-eyed look do not testify to a state of consciousness that has cut itself off from the refreshing, revitalizing, and life-issuing sources of deep consciousness—and, because of this, is spent.

In the past, a great deal was known about the *dynamics* of consciousness and the ways and means of bringing it to ever further stages of awakening; equally as much was certainly also known, however, about the meaning of the *sleep* of consciousness and about the ways and means of combating that sleeplessness. Thus in the Taoist texts, and particularly in the *Tao Te Ching* of Lao Tzu, we find a wealth of insights into the constructive and healing effect of inactivity, of silence, of retreat, as means of making space for something higher than one's current consciousness to prevail. And that "something higher" is nothing else than the efficacy of the deeper layers of consciousness, which belong to the realm of sleep.

According to Lao Tzu, the great art and wisdom of the "ancients" consisted precisely in the fact that they did not want to "do" everything: they merely created inner and outer conditions such as would present no impediments to things *happening* of themselves in the right way.

> The Heaven and Earth join, and the sweet rain falls, beyond the command of men, yet evenly upon all.[8]

> I do nothing and people are reformed of themselves. I love quietude and the people are righteous of themselves.[9]

These passages from the *Tao Te Ching* contain the core of the problem of the correct relationship to sleep, and of "proper sleep." The "doing nothing" meant here is not inac-

[8] *Tao Te Ching*, 32 (Lin Yutang trsl).
[9] Ibid., 57.

tivity, but a renunciation of activity. It is the inner process in which the active waking consciousness leaves it to the deeper-lying forces of sleeping consciousness to perfect the work. In other words, it is the bringing-into-motion of the forces that are at work in sleeping consciousness. The result expected from this rearrangement is that "the people are righteous of themselves." That is, by making space for the forces of transformation and growth to have their effect, just this sort of transformation and this sort of growth will take place in the realm of the "collective unconscious" (to use the expression of the depth psychologist C. G. Jung).

"Command" in the *Tao Te Ching*'s sense (in the above verse) is not rule by giving orders, but ordering[10] and guiding by renouncing rulership, by leaving the work of ruling to a power before which we retreat, before which we bow, just as *consciously* as "the people" follow it out of free inclination (that is, "of themselves"). True ruling, in the *Tao Te Ching*'s sense, is ruling through inclination, not through compulsion. Only those are rulers who have renounced command and compulsion, those whose deepest heart-forces manifest as the peoples' free inclinations. This is the ideal ruler of the *Tao Te Ching*. But it is at the same time the idea of Christ the King, as it lives in the Catholic Church.

Christ the King is not the king who rules by means of power; He is, rather, the king of hearts. It is impossible for anyone who has a heart not to love Him. And anyone who loves Him will not wish for, or be capable of, anything other than to serve Him. This is the meaning of the idea of Christ the King in the Catholic Church. Was it borrowed from Taoism? It has been borrowed neither from Taoism

---

[10] To "give orders": *ver-ordnen*. To "order": *ordnen*.

31

nor from any other school of thought. It is, rather, the expression of the deep human moral consciousness that has progressed from obedience out of fear to service out of love.

The correct relationship in consciousness to the realm of sleep (i.e., the correct relationship between waking and sleeping consciousness) would be realized if: on the one hand, waking consciousness were to become ever more awake as a result of drawing upon the refreshing, rejuvenating sources of sleeping consciousness; and, on the other, sleeping consciousness were to become ever more deeply asleep by incorporating the concepts, ideas, and ideals of waking consciousness in such a way into its calm, constructive, nurturing processes that they become essential orienting powers therein.

Thus a consequent Idealist (a Hegelian, say)[11] believes that only an all-embracing system, all of whose members relate to each other without contradiction and require each other with logical necessity, can be true; and consequently, that it is a matter of constructing just such a system in consciousness in order then to incorporate any given experience into it. Experience teaches us, however, that such a system, once it is in all essentials built, quickly becomes an exhausting burden, loses its fruitfulness, and in the end brings on a mood of boredom. Such a consciousness grows patently bored.

Why does the all-embracing system of a philosophical worldview exhaust consciousness? The answer lies in the fact that the correct relationship between waking and sleep-

---

[11] I.e., a "waking consciousness" thinker in whom the "correct relationship between waking and sleeping consciousness" is compromised, as pointed out in the next paragraph.

ing consciousness has been compromised. For by constructing a system bent on satisfying *its* requirements (its logical requirements, at least), waking consciousness has fabricated a "unity" out of the world's apparent multiplicity. But the world's unity, which is indeed in itself absolutely undeniable (given that if there were no such unity, no cognition would be either possible or conceivable), is not merely something that makes the world *conceivable*, but is something that *holds the world together and shapes it into a real and effective unity.* When I breathe the air, and my bitterest enemy does the same, the *reality* of our connectedness is revealed in a quite different way than it is in the *concept* "human being" under which both my enemy and I are classified. He and I may also have the most opposite intuitions possible, and may value opposite things; but birth, toil, suffering, and death nevertheless make us companions in fate.

The governing unity of the world is not the same as the "unity" of some conceptual system we might construct for ourselves concerning the world. The governing unity lies in a different realm than does the systematizing activity of consciousness. It lies in the realm of our sleeping consciousness. From there it does indeed *effect* the harmony of our individual cognitions, but without *itself* ever being able to become an individual cognition or a system—even were this individual cognition to have the whole world as its object! For even an all-comprehending system can at best offer only *one* aspect of the world, and for this reason can only make the world comprehensible from *one* point of view. If this were not so, the system in question would have at the same time to be a philosophical system, a drama of worlds, a symphony, a religious mystery-cult, and perhaps many other things as well. But there is no system of this kind, nor can there ever be, for such a system is not "native" to the realm of waking consciousness, but to that of sleeping consciousness. We sleep in the whole; we are awake in the part.

But sleeping need not be fruitless, just as waking is not always fruitful. The sleeping consciousness, the consciousness veiled in darkness, is not without its effect. It gathers up the experiences and cognitions of waking consciousness into an organic unity. What I have acquired in my waking consciousness through individual experiences and cognitions is, by and by, brought into concord out of my sleeping consciousness—brought into concord, that is, "of themselves." The great synthesis of all individual things happens there "of themselves." Or, as the *Tao Te Ching* pictorially expresses this process: "The Heaven and Earth join, and the sweet rain falls, beyond the command of men, yet evenly upon all."

The great unity, the "joining of Heaven and Earth," permits an effect to proceed from itself which, without any guidance from human consciousness, creates peace ("sweet rain"). It binds together unconnected items of experience and knowledge which, by and by, are shaped as if of their own accord into an organic whole free from contradiction. Facts of experience, results of logical inferences, psychological insights, moral postulates, and aesthetic valuations join together in this way in a harmonious unity whose individual members complete and illuminate each other. The connection of these individual experiences and cognitions—a connection hidden behind them, its *composition*—emerges out of the deep realm of the sleeping consciousness into the light with growing clarity.

The *knowing* of waking consciousness is transformed by the sleeping consciousness into *wisdom*. This transformation happens "of itself," but its fruits, its results, may not materialize in waking consciousness if that consciousness has not learned to abide in stillness and patience at the threshold of sleeping consciousness—if it does not let the waves coming from beyond this threshold flow through it. These waves leave behind in waking consciousness not only a refreshing and rejuvenating effect, but also many an insight into the deeper connection of things previously present in consciousness, but in an apparently unconnected way.

The conscious intercourse of waking consciousness with sleeping consciousness must be learned. This learning means achieving a higher measure of wakefulness—a wakefulness, however, that is calm and without any object. It is a matter of remaining at the threshold of waking consciousness without slipping over into the realm of sleep, of remaining awake in an objectless consciousness that hearkens to the silence, that is turned to look into the darkness—i.e., that stands facing that which is without object.

⊕

The conscious regulation of the relation between waking consciousness and sleeping consciousness is just as important to the health of consciousness as a harmonious relationship between sleeping and waking is to the health of the body. And true openness, true freedom from prejudice, is also part of the health-bringing consequences of a regulated relationship between the waking and sleeping layers of consciousness. We mean by this an open attitude towards each new experience and a willingness to arrive at insights in completely new ways—all the while accompanied by a calm, even carefree, readiness to leave it to the deeper layers of consciousness to bring these new experiences and these new ways of arriving at insights into harmony with earlier experiences and with ways tried earlier.

Leaving it to the activity of sleeping consciousness to gather up our different experiences and cognitions into a "system" brings about a freedom of movement and a mobility in consciousness that is otherwise constricted—indeed often made impossible—by the sort of system or methodology constructed by waking consciousness. A consciousness that has essentially given over "systematizing" activity to the sleeping consciousness is free, for example, to think about psychological phenomena using purely psychological concepts and according to purely psychological methods; to judge scientific problems using scientific concepts and according to scientific methods; to investigate theological topics in a theological way; and so on. Such a consciousness will guard itself against bringing or interpreting mechanical ideas into psychology. It will guard itself against expecting moral results from mechanical ideas, against replacing the moral with the aesthetic, against seeking religion along the paths of rational argument alone. It will guard itself against applying *one* single method to *all* objects and fields of existence, for it will know from experience that on *this* side of the threshold of waking consciousness there is *multiplicity*, and that the *unity* of object and method belongs to the domain lying on the *other* side of that threshold.

Or, in Kant's terms: the "thing-in-itself" lies beyond experience and reason, even in the case of the "thing-in-itself" of the world as a whole. The "thing-in-itself" of the world, the world's "system," is a *unity*. It belongs to the realm of consciousness-in-itself, that is, to the realm of sleeping consciousness. By contrast, *multiplicity* of experience and reason ("pure reason") belong to the realm of waking consciousness. In other words: the "thing-in-itself" belongs to sleep; appearance belongs to waking. The correct relationship between sleeping and waking is at the same time the correct relationship between *essence* and *appearance*. This correct relationship is no other than the health of consciousness—or "wisdom."

Grace and Works. Such "wisdom" as we are speaking of can assuredly be found in the Chinese spiritual life of the past. But we meet it elsewhere. The Christian teaching on grace and works manifests this wisdom to an extraordinary degree, for everything in this traditional teaching as it lives on in the Catholic and Eastern Orthodox Churches tends towards bringing waking consciousness and sleeping consciousness into a relationship that is not only healthy but is also effective in outward healing.

When waking consciousness is active (when it is as awake as possible) it is the author of "works"—of efforts, exertions, deeds, achievements. Correlatively, sleeping consciousness, which is always present at the same time as waking consciousness, is the realm of the effects of "grace"—of constructive forces that bring about growth. These forces lie beyond the arbitrary will and the calculation of waking consciousness, and for this reason seem veiled in the darkness of the "sleep of consciousness." In other words, works are *carried out*, whereas grace *happens* of itself. Grace befalls us, and in this sense does *not* belong to our waking consciousness. It is not our "work." It belongs, rather, to the deeper or higher levels of sleeping consciousness, whose effects we certainly experience *in* waking consciousness, but which we cannot ourselves *bring about*. Grace, in the sense of the Christian tradition alive today, is so far independent of waking consciousness that we can justly say it lies outside us, that it belongs to the realm where waking consciousness is shut down: the realm of sleeping consciousness.

The correct relationship between waking and sleeping consciousness thus depends on understanding and living the relationship between grace and works. On this, however, also depends the health of consciousness, its capacity for wisdom. If, for example, we came to the view that works alone are definitive or significant, we might well set in motion a great bustle of activity in the world, but we would at the same time put our consciousness in a diseased state of sleeplessness. If on the other hand we came to the conviction that grace alone effectuates everything, in time we would so greatly diminish the activity of our waking consciousness that we would enter a diseased state of drowsiness.

As for the correct relationship between sleeping and waking as a task, it is indicated in the gospel formulas:

> Ask, and it shall be given you; seek, and ye shall find; knock, and it shall be opened unto you.

Seeking, knocking, and asking belong to waking consciousness, to the realm of *works*. By contrast, what is found, the opened door, and what is given, belong to the realm that lies beyond waking consciousness, the realm of *grace*.

Asking, as has just been said, is an activity of waking consciousness. But the "giving" that follows depends on the asking as little as water depends on thirst. These three formulas may be seen, rather, as the *seeds* from which, in the course of centuries, a many-branched tree of the doctrine of works and grace has grown. The branches assuredly grew their separate ways, and many withered over time. But the trunk of the tree lives on: it remains standing, ever the same. For however far we may wish to go within Christianity in depreciating human works, we can neither deny the Master's behests to "seek," "knock," and "ask," nor reinterpret them as their opposites. And likewise, however far we may wish to go in esteeming the merits and attainments of human works, we can neither deny the meaning of the Master's expressions "ye shall find," "it shall be opened unto you," and "it shall be given you," nor reinterpret them as their opposites.

Pelagianism, semi-Pelagianism, the Christian rationalism of a Tolstoy, Socinianism, Unitarianism, liberal Protestantism: they all undervalue grace. What they believe, in effect, is that those who knock open the door themselves: a spiritual breaking and entering! As for the predestinationism of Lucidus, Jan Hus, and Calvin, as well as Luther's doctrine of justification through faith alone and of the vanity of works: they all fall short in their estimation of works and of the human being from whom they flow. They believe that whoever opens the door also prearranged the knocking—in other words, that a prescripted piece of theater is being performed.

The underestimation of both grace and of works is underpinned by a demonstrably inaccurate estimation of human nature. The view that works are in themselves worthless rests on the notion that human nature is corrupt through and through, and thus in itself capable only of sin. Correlatively, the view that human nature is not in itself

corrupt (i.e., that the Fall has, or henceforth has, no reality)
rests on the notion that we need no supernatural action of
grace to realize our true vocation.

Now, the Church of tradition teaches that "nature is
wounded, but not destroyed" (*natura vulnerata, non deleta*),
and that, consequently, representatives both of pre-Christian humanity and of present-day non-Christian humanity,
were and are capable of works of justice, goodness, and wisdom. Or, as this conclusion is formulated in lapidary fashion in the seventh canon of the sixth session of the Council
of Trent:

> *Si quis dixerit opera omnia quae ante justificationem*
> *fiunt, quacumque ratione facta sint, vere esse peccata,*
> *anathema sit.*

> If anyone should assert that all works that were car-
> ried out before the justification were, irrespective of
> the reasons for which they were done, truly sins, let
> him be anathema.

Accordingly, the Jesuit missionaries to China in the seventeenth and eighteenth centuries came to the view that the
Chinese were in possession of the main elements of natural
religion (*religio naturalis*) and that they needed nothing
more than the supplementation of their religion through
divine revelation in order to participate in perfect truth,
both natural *and* revealed. On the other hand, everyone
who has looked around in the world knows from experience that not only highly civilized Chinese and Indians,
but also members of so-called "primitive peoples," often
show themselves to be of a moral integrity that puts Christians to shame.

Thus, a well-intentioned American visiting a Navajo reservation in the state of Arizona (this happened in the twentieth century) advised a member of the tribe to open a business offering for sale such daily staples as his fellow tribe members needed, so as to free them from the white traders who were profiting from them. The Navajo picked up on the idea. He got going, and brought the necessary goods into the reservation. He opened a business and sold the goods to his fellow tribe members... for the same price he had paid for them! When the well-intentioned American alerted him to the fact that this was not really the way to conduct a "business," the Navajo replied, "how can I ask from the people of my tribe more than I myself paid?" When the American answered that he, the Navajo, had undertaken work deserving of some reward, the Navajo said, "Should I ask my fellow tribe members to pay me money for making a journey of a few weeks and bringing them goods?" A salesman simply could not be made of him. Can it be believed that this Navajo had committed a sin by founding a non-profit business? Whoever asserts this, let him be anathema.

Just as experience teaches that human nature includes inherent traits of unspoiled nobility, so with the same certainty it also teaches that human nature displays traits of self-seeking, injustice, and cruelty. Can it be believed that a Grand Inquisitor, a Torquemada,[12] who was fully instructed in the religion of love, could at the behest of the God of love burn alive men who believed otherwise than himself? Whoever asserts this, let him be anathema.

---

[12] Tomás de Torquemada (1420–1498), Castilian Dominican friar and first Grand Inquisitor of the Spanish Inquisition.

Both historical and personal lived experience teach us that human nature is equally healthy and sick morally; in other words, that the principle *natura vulnerata, non deleta* is *true*. From this it follows that human nature is capable of being turned not only towards lying, hatred, and wickedness, but also of striving towards truth, beauty, and goodness. In other words, it is capable of "seeking," "knocking," and "asking."[13] Moreover, it also follows from this principle that human nature is in need of healing.

This healing requires the means of healing that lies outside human nature—grace. From the realization that human nature is at once healthy and sick, innocent and sinful, two things follow: that, as a revelation of innocent human nature, works are valuable; and that, as standing in need of the healing and the salvific effects of grace, it is necessary that its seeking should lead to a "finding," so that it "shall be opened" unto them, and so that it shall be "given" them!

Lastly, there follows from this principle something especially important here in connection with the problem of waking and sleeping: that the life of consciousness can only become healthy if it learns to be awake properly and to sleep properly, if it uses its own forces fully and correctly while at the same time learning to receptively abandon itself to, and to trust in, higher forces as if they were its own.

In this sense, the solution of the problem of "works *and* grace" offered by the Church of tradition is not only theologically true, is not only in accord with all life-experience, but *psycho-therapeutically* is also the solution to the problem of the health of consciousness as the concordant coopera-

---

[13] The manuscript has "answering" here.

42

tion between waking and sleeping, between activity and passivity of consciousness.

When does this cooperation of waking and sleeping consciousness happen to the highest degree? Or, in theological terms, when is the cooperation of nature and supernature, of "works" and "grace," most strongly experienced? This occurs in such deeds as emerge from a state of consciousness that is simultaneously one of perfect awakeness (even hyper-awakeness) and perfect sleep (even deepest sleep). These are deeds in which, while the whole consciousness is as bright as sunlight, midnight stillness and darkness pour out of this brightness; deeds in which all efforts and sacrifices are easy, accomplished as if "of themselves"; deeds in which we are as relaxed and natural as we are in deep sleep, as alert and awake as if bidding farewell on our death bed. Deeds that originate in this state of the greatest possible "of themselves," and of the greatest possible wakefulness, are deeds of *love*. Love is the state in which true awakening and true sleep are in perfect concord. In love, *doing* and *happening* are one. In love is revealed the *achievement* of the cooperating realms of waking and sleeping.

II

On Personal Certainty

HERE ARE QUESTIONS WHICH ARE LIKE HUNGER and thirst. They are part of what it is to be human, and can neither be talked nor decreed out of existence unless we have fallen victim to intellectual or moral idiocy. The origin and destiny of the world, the ruling principle or nature of the world, the nature of human personhood, its fate and its calling in life and in death, are questions of this kind. Is the world an endless sequence of events, without beginning and end, that automatically creates and also annihilates itself? Or does the world have a beginning and an end; i.e., does it share the fate of all its constituent parts? Is the world a pure creation out of nothing, or is it a work of art fashioned from pre-existing material, whether it be everlasting or temporal? Is the world an emanation: an outflow, exhalation, or word from a supramundane primordial being? Or might it be this primordial being's dream, which unfolds only in its consciousness, in which all the individual beings in the world are but dream figures dreamt by someone else? Or is what we call "world" not some single thing at all, but instead a drama in which two, three, or more worlds come together, each with its own origin, its own originator, its own destiny? Might there even be as many worlds as there are unities of consciousness or beings, so that each being is a world unto itself, whether everlasting or transitory? Is there but *one* final essence at the basis of this world or worlds? If so, is it indifferent towards the beings and events of the world? Or is it compassionate? Or, indeed, is it perchance intent upon disaster, torment, and destruction? And am I, as a human being, as a consciously thinking, feeling, willing, and recollecting person, only a temporary constellation made up of external forces, such as appears for a while like a rainbow, only to later vanish? Or is there even such a thing as personhood as an essential reality that endures? Is the person an instrument of external forces, a ball for the world's game? Or does the person have the capacity for self-determination? Are we human beings free, or completely determined?

All these questions have been posed for millennia, and people of all ages and in all countries have ever sought answers to them. Even today, people are occupied with these questions in all the countries of the world. From this fact it follows that these questions belong to the life of the human spirit as such, and that (at least at a certain stage in the development of consciousness) they represent an essential component of this life of the spirit. It also follows (from the stubborn persistence of these questions) that there is in us an insuperable faith in the possibility of their being answered, a faith that has survived for millennia.

But from all this it follows also that these questions have never yet been answered in a way that is universally valid and binding for *everyone*. Indeed, the history of these questions (the history, that is, of religion, philosophy, and science) leaves behind it the general impression that what matters is not so much that these questions should be *answered* as that we should be *answerable* to them; that working on these questions is an indispensable element in the spiritual life of humanity, an element that keeps this spiritual life alive.

Just as it would be preposterous to be disappointed in water on the grounds that, after having quenched our thirst today we thirst again tomorrow, so would it be preposterous to say that if after millennia it has never yet proven possible to answer these questions in a universally valid way, answering them must represent a hopeless undertaking. Such a conclusion would be preposterous because, had these efforts always proved absolutely unsuccessful, the millennia-old efforts of human beings to answer these questions would long ago have been given up. The thirst *was* quenched, and quenched many times for many people. It is only that it was never quenched in a *universally valid* way—in a way that is binding for *everyone*. Thirst is a personal matter, as is its quenching.

⊕

In such matters, we experience personal *uncertainty*, whereas what we seek is to arrive at personal *certainty* concerning them. Personal certainty *has* been attained by many people, in all ages. It is only that this achievement did not spare *other* people the need to arrive at personal certainty *for themselves*. Indeed, not only has personal certainty been attained in all ages: it has also always *intensified*. For there is no limit to the intensification, to the growth, of certainty, just as there is apparently also no limit to the possibility of uncertainty, insecurity, and doubt.

Under some circumstances we can intensify our personal certainty infinitely. But we can also drown in the shoreless ocean of doubt. There is only one thing we *cannot* do: we

47

cannot *compel* other people to understand. We cannot compel them to arrive at personal certainty about these questions, whether by force, by argument, or by method. It has never yet been possible to find answers to questions about God, humanity, and the world in a way that is binding for *all* people. What *has* long been found possible thousands upon thousands of times, however, is for *individuals* to arrive at different degrees of personal certainty about these questions.

⊕

This, in essence, is what Immanuel Kant said to humanity in his *Critique of Pure Reason* and his *Critique of Practical Reason*. He showed that, whereas there are no universally valid answers—binding for everyone—to questions about God, freedom, and immortality (*Critique of Pure Reason*), there *is* a path to personal certainty if we but permit the deep strata of moral life to speak within us. Furthermore, he showed that these strata *do* testify to the reality of God, freedom, and immortality in a convincing way (*Critique of Practical Reason*).

Kant's appeal—beyond reason, to the deeper nature of the human being, in order to come to certainty about questions of this kind—is especially significant. This is because it points to the thesis about the fundamental conditions of personal certainty that follows from our earlier reflections on waking and sleeping: i.e., that *true personal certainty is the result of the agreement of the waking consciousness with the deeper, or sleeping, consciousness.*

In other words: true personal certainty is the total result of experience as a whole, which is acquired in and through all the capacities of the human being—both active and passive. Personal certainty is a state in which knowing and conscience,[1] in which thinking, feeling, and willing have in their own way arrived at the same result and are in unison with each other.

As long as one sticks to the "logical truth," to laying-out a logically systematic worldview with the help of the seven-league boots of logic (a system that may be as clear as daylight to waking consciousness, but is also correspondingly *shallow*, leaving the deeper strata of consciousness undisturbed and uninvolved and thereby dispensing with *depth*), a deep-laid dissatisfaction, a persistent background nagging of profound underlying doubts, will always accompany assent to this system. Why? Because the deeper consciousness we refer to here cannot be excluded; its voice will not be absent. Its critical voice will wordlessly, continually, repeat: "not bread, but a stone."

It is not enough that what is held to be true should be *correct*; it must also be *profound*. Correctness does not suffice to bring about true personal certainty; profundity also belongs to that certainty. Only what is "true" both for waking and for sleeping consciousness is true—i.e., that which corresponds not only to the demands of thinking but also to those of feeling, willing, conscience, and perhaps of still deeper strata of consciousness.

Personal certainty is present, and is all the stronger, the more certain conditions are met. The content of what one is certain of:

—must be thinkable, feelable, and willable;

[1] "Knowing": *Wissen*. "Conscience": *Gewissen*.

—must be simultaneously true, beautiful, and good;

—must be *fruitful* for the life of thought, feeling, and the will, i.e., must possess a heuristic value;

—must have the effect of broadening the soul, and give impetus to moral life. For anything that does not give impetus to moral life is not beautiful and not true; anything that does not broaden the heart is not good and not true; anything that does not lead to further knowledge is not good and not beautiful;

—must make the whole human being *healthier* in spirit, soul, and body; i.e., clearer, calmer, more compassionate and more balanced;

—must rest either on personal experience, on the extension of personal experience by means of analogy, or on the experience of other persons regarding whom one's personal experience of their moral qualities and healthiness allow their testimony to be as trustworthy as if it were the testimony of one's own experience, or perhaps even more trustworthy.

Those who insist solely on their own authority block off many sources of stimulation and knowledge. Just as individuals are reliant for their experience on the working together of several different organs and capacities of consciousness, so are they also reliant on working together with other people in order that their experience may be broadened and their knowledge tested.

If I have a friend whom I trust as I trust myself, I have four eyes instead of two. If I have an honest opponent who rejects what I prize and prizes the opposite, I have a reason and an opportunity to put myself in that person's place, and to inspect my intuitions seriously and honestly. If, once the inspection is completed, my intuitions remain intact, they will have gained a greater measure of personal certainty, and I will have my honest opponent to thank for this. But when two or more people who have worked separately for many years on the same problems meet, and exchange, then do mutual growth, enrichment, and confirmation take place—and human collaboration celebrates its feast-day! When one holds an old book or manuscript in one's hands and suddenly experiences an encounter with a spiritual brother from the past (at first like a greeting from a distant past, but coming ever closer, ever more alive), then the author's voice becomes ever more perceptible until, astonished, one lays aside the book or manuscript and hears oneself say: *Exspecto resurrectionem mortu-orum.*[2]

Only solitary, independent seekers know the true value of collaboration, of commerce with contemporaries, of encountering people from past times, for they do not come with empty hands: they have something to exchange, to extend, to test. Encounters with people and books are to such seekers *events* on their life's way.

Quantitative life, or burying oneself in books and taking part in all manner of meetings and groups, does not lead to true collaboration: this is more like converting a banknote into small change. If it is justified to say *timeo hominem unius libri* ("I fear the man who sticks to one book alone")[3] it is no less justified to say *timeo hominem multitudinis librorum* ("I fear the bibliophile"). If the former is dangerous because he is always ready to cast a stone, the latter is

---

[2] "I look forward to the resurrection of the dead…" (Nicene Creed)
[3] Quotation attributed to St. Thomas Aquinas.

dangerous because he has put literature between himself and the world: for him, the means have become an end.

Not that reading should be little prized! Let us read! Let us, if possible, read a great deal. But let us read a book as, the evening before giving his verdict, a judge reads the statements of the witnesses and the accounts of the case given by the prosecution and defence; or as a doctor reads his patient's medical notes before deciding whether surgery is needed; or even as an intelligence officer reads messages sent by an enemy prisoner of war in order to discover indications of the enemy's strength, position, technical capabilities, and intentions, and to exploit these indications by careful comparison. In other words: only reading that is *intensive*, that happens for the sake of *practice*, is of use to the seeker of personal certainty. Practice is everything in life. Practice of the path to personal certainty in the great questions of the human race is no less a practice than those of justice, medicine, or war.

Books truly are to be taken seriously, for they provide the possibility of contact and collaboration with other people, living or dead. And yet it should never be forgotten that what matters is not books, but the world and life. Books can be either an important means of moving closer to reality, or an obstacle on the way. Seekers after true personal certainty will learn to estimate correctly the significance of books, just as they learn to estimate correctly the significance of relationships with people, of solitary musing, of observing what falls out in life, of psychological introspection, and of many other things besides.

The highest measure of personal certainty is attained when logical thinking says "yes" to it; when moral judgment or conscience says "yes" to it; when all our internal and external experience says "yes" to it; when aesthetic judgment or the sense of beauty says "yes" to it; when the bodily and spiritual sense of health says "yes" to it; when it is also recognized or championed by serious, clear-thinking, honest, and balanced people of the present and past whom with good reason we respect.

Personal certainty is the fruit of total knowledge: knowledge not only with our whole being but with all the beings whom we trust as much as, or more than, we trust ourselves.

III

Uncompelled Knowledge:
Science, Logic, Personal Certainty

RUE PERSONAL CERTAINTY IS THE RESULT OF THE cooperation of the waking consciousness and the deeper consciousness: "sleeping" consciousness. This means, among other things, that the occasion of knowledge leading to personal certainty consists of two simultaneous events: the *exertions* of the waking consciousness to learn many things in many ways, and the *growth* of personal certainty in breadth and depth. What is essential is not "acquisition" or "achievement" but a "growing into" personal certainty. What is *alive*, as truth, in such certainty, is not made or built by the seeking and laboring consciousness, but comes up freely of its own accord from the seeds sown in the *soil* of consciousness by those exertions—seeds whose origin lies beyond the waking consciousness.

It might be more accurate to say that it is not the seeking consciousness that discovers truth as personal certainty but it is truth that finds the soil of consciousness in which it can unfold. This unfolding happens *freely*, unchecked by the programatic intentions of consciousness or influences from the surroundings.

Freedom is the element in which personal certainty grows

regarding the questions that matter to the life of humanity. In other words, personal certainty arises in a way that can be thought of as *non-mechanical*. The mechanical is the element furthest removed from freedom. The mechanical is distinct from freedom in the way a machine is distinct from a plant. The machine functions; the plant lives. The machine was assembled; the plant unfolded from a seed.

Freedom consists precisely in the fact that an unrestricted or uncompelled unfolding of a being's own nature takes place. I am free if my nature, like a plant seed, unfolds unconstrained and without restriction. But I am unfree if my consciousness functions according to a system compiled, or *made*, whether by myself or by anyone else. The mechanization of consciousness, and especially of the capacity to think, can go very far—at least as far as the performance capacity of a machine for calculating and reacting (so-called artificial intelligence) can go. It is entirely possible, in principle, that a large number of logical presuppositions could be built into a machine, and that through a protocol of mechanical permutations this machine could draw an even greater number of logical inferences from those presuppositions. The achievements of such a machine would be unimpeachably correct, even if exceedingly superficial.

But it would not occur to any person to want to arrive at certainty concerning God, the soul, immortality, and freedom with the help of such a machine—as it will not itself ever be able to supply, take away, or weaken even the tiniest experience. The questions "Do elephants exist? Do the sun and stars exist? Do angels and demons exist?" will be irrelevant for this machine. It simply will not react to these questions. *Values*, too, such as good and evil, beautiful and ugly, and so on, will lie outside its capacity to function. To this machine, everything *qualitative* will be alien.

In the case, however, of consciousness seeking certainty about God, the soul, immortality, and freedom, it is precisely a matter of whether they *exist* and how they are procured, i.e., of *experience* and *quality*. Without experience and the evaluation of experience there can be no personal certainty. At issue is only what *kind* of experience and what *kind* of evaluation lead to personal certainty. The present chapter is devoted to this question.

When considering this question, what matters in the first place is to get clarity about the relationship between the path to personal certainty (which is a result of the "knowing" of the total human being) on the one hand, and about science and the scientific method on the other. A point of departure for attaining this clarity can be found by comparing the concept of "knowing" in the scientific sense and "certainty" in the sense of a personal experience of being certain.[1] Something "is known" in science when what "is known" is universally valid and necessary, i.e., is logically and experientially *binding* for every healthy adult. (There can be no "I know" in science, for to say "I know" is entirely irrelevant, scientifically speaking, and has as little to do with scientific knowledge as does the fact that I might have a cold or be in a good mood.)

What is binding and universal in scientific knowledge rests upon the selection and use of just three of the human being's capacities and domains of experience: logical think-

---

[1] "Knowing": *Wissen*. "Certainty": *Gewissheit*.

ing; external sensory experience (the claim to scientificity of the *internal* senses is disputed, i.e., the claim of psychological introspection); and memory, which conserves the results of logic and external sensory experience. All other human capacities and experiential domains, such as imagination and dreaming, conscience, the sense of health, the religious sense, the metaphysical sense, the sense of secrets, empathy, intuition, and so on, can certainly be *objects* of scientific knowledge, but cannot be a *means* to it.

The selection of logical thinking, of external sensory experience, and of memory as means of acquiring scientific knowledge reflects the scientific ideal of universal validity and necessity, and has its foundation in this ideal. For even if relatively few people are willing and able to *undertake* scientific research, the *results* of this research are nevertheless of a kind that they can be verified and found to be convincingly conclusive by any healthy adult.

Johann Baptista van Helmont (c. 1577–1644), for example, established scientifically that the material of which a plant consists is drawn largely from the air, by putting a willow branch weighing five pounds in a large pot together with two hundred pounds of dry earth, preventing any dust from settling on the earth in the pot, watering the earth in the pot for five years with rainwater alone, and after those five years establishing that the willow weighed 164 pounds (around 82 pounds in a dry state), while the earth in the pot had lost only two ounces of dry weight. In this way everyone, whether Catholic, Protestant, Jew, or agnostic, was compelled to acknowledge that an increase in the dry weight of the willow of about eighty pounds had *not* happened at the expense of the soil in the pot but at that of the air and/or the water. Today, we know that the eighty pounds contain about thirty pounds of carbon. Even if the remaining fifty pounds of water and oxygen come from the rainwater, the thirty pounds of carbon can only be taken from the air, and indeed from the carbon dioxide in the air. Anyone who might doubt this is free to repeat the experiment.

Further experiments in the direction pioneered by van Helmont led to more such results. Thus Liebig (1840)[2] established that carbon dioxide, water, and ammonia contain the elements needed to make a plant. Boussingault (1855)[3] showed that plants could thrive in a soil from which all the organic matter had been removed by combustion, just as long as nitrogenous matter (nitrates) was added to the water in the soil. From this demonstration it follows that the air is the only possible source of the carbon taken in by the plant, and that plants are not normally able to extract the substance contained in the air directly from the air. Boussingault and Dumas (1860–1890)[4] also showed that the green leaves of plants absorb the carbon in the air when exposed to sunlight, and that they gain correspondingly in dry weight. Finally, Sachs (1884)[5] calculated that a sunflower

---

[2] Justus von Liebig (1803–1873). The year 1840 cited here refers to the year of publication of Liebig's work, *Die organische Chemie in ihrer Anwendung auf Agricultur und Physiologie* (Braunschweig, 1840).

[3] Jean Baptiste Boussingault (1802–1887). The year 1855 cited here likely refers to that author's article published that year: "De l'Action du Salpêtre sur la Végétation" (*Comptes rendus hebdomadaires des séances de l'Académie des sciences*, Band 41, 845–75).

[4] Boussingault collaborated around the year 1840 with the chemist Jean Baptiste André Dumas (1800–1844), as indicated in the work *Essai de statique chimique des êtres organisés* (Paris, 1842). It is unclear why Tomberg cites here "1860–1890," since both scientists died before 1890.

[5] Julius Sachs (1832–1884) published the findings cited here in the periodical *Arbeiten*, of the Botanical Institute of Würzburg.

with a leaf surface area of 1.5 square meters gains about 36 grams in dry weight a day when exposed to sunlight.

In this way, step by step, knowledge of the conditions and sequence of events in so-called "photosynthesis" was arrived at—that is, knowledge of the astonishing event of the transformation of inorganic into organic matter, of carbon dioxide into starch and sugar, taking place within the plant. Whenever we enjoy sweet grape juice today, we know that the grape sugar it contains comes largely from the carbon dioxide in the air, and that it is a result of the interaction between sunlight and the green leaf of the plant. The sun and the plant transform the inorganic into the organic; they transform "stone" into "bread." This is a valuable result of the scientific method of questioning observation and answering experiment.

We owe many results of the greatest value to this method of "intelligent empiricism." These results are as universally valid and binding as are the intelligently handled *facts* upon which they are based. Here it is a case of a causally or temporally ordered phenomenology. This is why the empirical results of a science directed towards a well-ordered phenomenology (however binding they might be) are just as welcome and as worthy of glad and free acceptance as any hints or clues towards the solution of a riddle are welcome to a person struggling to solve it.

⊕

But the concern of science as it is really experienced is not confined to the empirical-phenomenological mode. It has also a theoretical foundation and superstructure. Its theoretical foundation is provided by the presuppositions of natural science, which are themselves not of an empirical and phenomenological order, but constitute instead the "creed" of science. As for the superstructure, it consists of the theories put forward as hypotheses. The founding principles of natural science—the creed or confession of faith, if you will, that lies at the basis of modern natural science as its presupposition—can be brought back to the following sentence: "Everything that happens, does so according to laws, and these laws are fashioned in such a way that we can discover them." In other words, science presupposes that there is a discoverable order in the world; that this order, or these laws, can be discovered as the universal "remaining balance" after the method of abstraction has stripped away the world's individual appearances; and that this remaining balance (the world order) is precisely the goal of science. The method of abstraction, that is, *abstracting* from individuals to discover the general, and from other groups of appearances to investigate a *particular* group for its own sake, and *generalizing* further beyond the bounds of current human experience (the inductive method for arriving at universal judgments), all presuppose the belief that abstraction does not distort reality, and that generalization (making judgments about the whole world on the basis of five, ten, or a thousand individual phenomena observed or subjected to experiment) is possible and justified.

A third belief held by science, or rather by scientists, is that of the *simplicity* of nature. This belief that what is simplest is also what is most natural, when adopted as obedience to a methodological device, goes back to Ockham's "razor," *pluralitas non est ponenda sine necessitate ponendi.*[6]

---

[6] "Entities should not be multiplied beyond necessity," often paraphrased as "the simplest explanation is usually the best one."

Scientists, however, go well beyond this methodological device: they elevate the principle of simplicity into a criterion for choosing among two or more conceivable systems of order that are equally adequate to the facts of sensory experience. The Ptolemaic theory of the solar system, for example, was just as "scientific" as that of Copernicus. Its drawback consisted solely in the fact that the Copernican theory was less complicated. The Copernican theory made it possible to explain in a mathematically *simpler* way the same facts the Ptolemaic theory expressed in a mathematically more complex way, even if the latter accounted for those facts equally well.[7]

The postulate of simplicity also stands behind scientists' attempts to reduce the multiplicity of the world to a single "substance" or material, to something non-composite and simple that fills space and effectuates motion therein, including as well such forms of "motion" as growth and consciousness. This is the ideal of those scientific thinkers who hope to reduce all sciences to physics. It is their ideal because in physics the principle of simplicity has become the ruling and unifying principle. This principle of simplicity has taken on greater validity in physics than elsewhere because it is in physics that the greatest approximation to the ideal of mathematical exposition has been achieved. For in the end, the scientific ideal consists first in reducing the world to a series of equations with several unknowns, then further reducing these equations to a *single* equation with just one unknown, and then calculating this unknown, i.e., expressing it in terms of known quantities.

[7] Cf. L.S. Stebbing, *A Modern Introduction to Logic* (London), 296–98. VT

Max Planck showed that this ideal could only be attained through the exclusion of anthropomorphic elements from science.[8] He did this by positing that definitions of tone, color, and temperature in physics no longer have anything in common with immediate perceptions of the individual senses. For him, tone and color are defined in terms of the frequency and wavelength of oscillations, and temperature is either measured theoretically on an absolute temperature scale (corresponding to the second law of thermodynamics) or is defined as the kinetic energy of molecular movements in a gas. In all such definitions nothing remains of the feeling of warmth, of seeing, or of hearing. In this way we are led to the paradox that what is *known* by means of immediate experience is *explained* by means of unknown things beyond experience!

The paradox implicit in this scientific development is obvious enough. But it becomes all the more dubious when not only color, tone, and warmth, but also events in consciousness such as thinking, feeling, and willing, are equally conceived as "epiphenomenal" appearances handily reduced to electrical discharges and oscillations in the nervous system or to chemical reactions set in motion by the internal secretions of glands.

The reduction of consciousness to something mechanical and chemical is as patently dubious as it is methodologically nonsensical, since, *given that consciousness is primary*, all experience arises in consciousness and on the presupposition of a consciousness. The reduction of consciousness to extra-conscious factors, factors discovered (or more often

---

[8] Max Plank, *A Survey of Physics* (London, 1925), 5. VT

invented!) by this same consciousness, is methodologically equivalent to trying to explain what exists by means of what does not exist, to explain light by means of darkness, warmth by means of cold, life by means of death.

Yes, taking our start from the givenness and direct experience of consciousness, we can speak of a reduced "quantity" of consciousness—that is, along the lines of a "dreaming," a "sleeping," and even (approaching the limiting zero-point) a "purely latent" consciousness—but we *cannot* take our start in the opposite direction by having consciousness take its origin from the absence of consciousness.

Put another way, the minimum of a quality may conceivably be *deduced* from its maximum; but it is unthinkable that the maximum should *derive* from the minimum, or indeed from non-existence. For this reason, the proposition that mechanical forces such as electricity have "worked their way up" into willing, into feeling, and in the end even into thinking, simply cannot be thought. It is an abdication of thinking. Moreover, it is also an abdication of experience, since the transition from something mechanical to something conscious can itself never be the content of an experience.

The epiphenomenal explanation of consciousness put forward by so many scientists belongs in fact neither to the empirical-phenomenological results of science nor to its theoretical foundation. It is, rather, an example of the transfer to the domain of science of what is in truth a methodological principle of unity and simplicity drawn from the domain of metaphysics. It is among the hypotheses that make up what we may call the *superstructure* of science. Taken as a whole, these hypotheses represent the so-called "scientific worldview." They contain possible, probable, and "almost certain" answers to questions about the origin, nature, and future of the world. This worldview is no other than the result of the generalization of particular research results of physics, chemistry, biology, and astronomy: it is the metaphysical flower that has grown in the soil of these sciences.

Before we delve further into this scientific worldview, it is fitting that we first address the question as to whether its teachings can in fact *themselves* be investigated scientifically (i.e., whether its teachings can be investigated in a universally valid and binding way). In other words, it will be appropriate to inquire how far the scientific method can be extended into a worldview without giving up the actual "scientificity" of its results—without giving up, that is, their universal validity and necessity.

No one will deny that propositions such as "the sum of the angles of a triangle is equal to two right angles" or "a part is smaller than the whole" are distinguished, by their certainty, from propositions such as "the climate in England is mild," or "fire warms." Statements about *states of fact* are certain in a quite different sense than are mathematical and logical propositions. The latter are *true* in themselves, whereas statements about states of fact can be either *true* or *false* in themselves: they rely on experience. Now, all statements in natural science belong to the category of statements of fact. They are acquired by *inductive* reasoning.

⊕

From the standpoint of logic, the inductive method rests on a *simple enumeration* of the objects of experience and the *formation of hypotheses* resulting from it. The proposition "all ravens are black" is the result of repeated experience (the observation of black ravens) *and* of the hypothesis that all the other ravens not yet observed must also be black.

Precisely formulated, the proposition would run as follows: "All the ravens observed were black; consequently, all ravens are black." Or, still more precisely: "observed raven 1, raven 2, raven 3, raven 4..., raven *n*, were black; consequently, raven *n* + 1, raven *n* + 2, raven *n* + 3..., or *all* ravens, will be black." Here, however, it is assumed that the ravens observed are *not* all the ravens that exist; thus, from the premise of *some* ravens, an inference is made to *all* ravens. This inference is formally invalid. In our present example, it is also *materially* invalid, since from time to time we come across white or so-called albino ravens.

Within the parameters of our example, then, the most we can say as a result of the inductive method (that is, by inference from the whole to the part) is: "all the ravens observed were black; consequently, it is (more or less) *probable* that all ravens are black."

Formally, there is a false inference in concluding that a given hypothesis is true because all the consequences drawn from it have so far turned out to be true. When, for example, someone says: "If a son hates his father, he will dream that he wants to murder him; consequently, if the son has dreamed that he wants to murder his father, he must hate his father," it is a case of making the false inference of "asserting the conclusion" (*ponendi consequentem*). The conclusion that "the son must hate his father" could only be validly drawn if no other premises than the one given could lead to the same inference.[9] In our example, however,

---

[9] Cf. Stebbing, *Introduction to Logic,* 104–6, 408 ff. VT

this is not the case, since the son might just as easily be living in fear of committing a sin, in which case the dream would be an expression of what he fears rather than an expression of what he wishes for. Furthermore, in the case of a nightmare rather than of a dream of wish-fulfillment, the very opposite conclusion could be drawn: that the son had a patricidal dream precisely because he loved and respected his father.

Induction, then, is not a valid method of inference unless it is taken merely in the sense of inferring what is possible and probable. But statements that are merely possible or probable cannot be *scientific* results, i.e., they cannot be taken as binding and universally valid. They may have a perfectly justified function as "working hypotheses" within the household of scientific research; but if they claim a significance beyond this in the realm of an overall worldview, they enter the field as co-contenders with the metaphysical doctrines of philosophy and religion, and thus fall within the criteria and requirements that apply in *that* field.

Every scientific hypothesis that becomes a theory which claims to buttress a worldview drops thereby out of the field of science and loses the protection of science. Henceforth it must meet the logical, moral, aesthetic, and other requirements that pertain in this metaphysical domain. For here its claim to scientificity is no longer valid. Here it must *earn* recognition, not by means of its scientificity (for induction cannot result in a scientific metaphysics), but instead by means of its *value* for the intellectual life of humanity: it must show itself to be a contribution to wisdom, goodness, and beauty, or else be rejected and forgotten as being shallow, fruitless, and crude. This goes as well for the entire superstructure of natural science that has been erected as a complex of hypothetical worldviews on the basis of the empirical-phenomenological results of scientific research.

As an aid to understanding, we may picture the entirety of this superstructure of natural science as a cosmic "family-tree"[10] representing the theory of perfectibility (of evolution) that arises from the humblest origins and is said to explain how, over the course of millennia, higher beings have developed from the lower. This development (so it is said) contains within itself first and foremost an immanent tendency to develop from the simple to the differentiated and complex; secondly, an opposite tendency to copy and retain (the principle of heredity); and thirdly, a capacity to adapt to changes in the environment, which capacity is opposed in its turn to the second tendency.

It does not make much difference whether the very beginning (the "root" of the cosmic family-tree) is thought of along with the physicists as an electrical field moving from a neutral to a polarized state, leading in turn to the first electrons (or other components of the atomic nucleus), which then integrate themselves to make up the *original atom*; or whether this very beginning is thought of with the biologists as an *original cell*. Both the physicists' original atom and the biologists' original cell tend *in some way* either to become parts of a complex whole or to become more complex themselves.

Without this immanent tendency (whether of a mechanical and dynamic, or a biological and purposive kind), one

[10] *Kosmische Stammbaum.* Rather than "family-tree," in philosophical and scientific contexts, *Stammbaum* carries the more particular meaning of "lineage," "phylogenetic" tree or table, or "genealogical" tree or table.

cannot conceive why and how the original atoms would not simply go on existing as unassuming original atoms; or why the original cells would not go on existing for all eternity as contented original cells. But then again, even such an unassuming, contented living-on (let alone the "development to higher stages" of the original atom, or of the original cell) is itself inconceivable without a continually repeating process of *generation*, i.e., without some kind of *reproduction* that keeps copying them. For the original atoms must otherwise have long since have exhausted their original charge of energy; and likewise, over time the original cells must unavoidably have fallen victim to the same fate. A continual *renewal*, repeated millions and millions of times, both of the atoms' energy and of the overall structure of the cells, must be thought of *as already present* in the first moments of their existence, i.e., as actually simultaneous with their first appearance.

But even the reproduction or renewal of the original atoms and the original cells does not suffice to make conceivable any sort of *changes* in the original atoms' and cells' structure, or in their relationship to each other. For it is a case, to be sure, not only of a *single* atom or of a *single* cell, swimming alone in an atomless sea of energy or in a cell-less sea of inorganic matter. The assumption is that the atom or cell was not alone, but encountered others. This encounter of atoms or of cells (which we are thinking of as the most primitive stage) can only mean one of three things: they *glided past* each other without making any impression or having any influence on each other; they *combined* with each other and thereafter continued on together; or they *opposed* or collided with each other.

Simply gliding past each other does not lead to any further history, for if that was all that ever happened, the original state of the world would have remained unchanged. If combining with each other was all that ever happened, the combined cells would in time have formed a single, massive, cosmic clump of cells, a colony; and the combined atoms would have formed an enormous cosmic mass of inorganic matter. If colliding with each other was all that ever happened, such collisions could never have led to today's world of planetary and organic forms, since the colliding atoms and cells would either have annihilated each other, or would have repelled each other to such a distance that the world would be imaginable only as the most rarefied sort of gaseous matter.

⊕

An ability to *adapt* must therefore be imagined (at least for the original cells). Indeed, this must be an ability to adapt such as includes the following other capacities: a kind of *perception* of events or of changes in the environment; an ability to *move* on the basis of such perception and enter into or avoid a relationship of associative combination or of opposition; and a kind of ability to *learn*, to retain experiences of this kind even if only in the form of a reflex and to pass this capacity on to descendants.

These capacities are the *minimum* the original cell would have had to possess in order to render even remotely conceivable any "development" from the primitive, single-celled, living being to a complicated organism such as a human being. Let us hear what biologist Edgar Dacqué (1878–1945) had to say about this:

As soon as we imagine even the most primitive living being, even if we only ascribe to it the minimum our actual experience allows (that is, if we are still to speak of it as a living being at all and not as a merely material and organic lump of slime), then what we have left is that which natural science came to think of as the first living beings, which came about by a process of abiogenesis,[11] and which it even suspected of having existed for an age at the bottom of the ocean, as a gelatinous precipitate, until the present day. Such a being must possess a body consisting of organic substance, which, however formless it might be, cannot fail to have a certain inner, more or less inert, individual coherence that it so correlates as to sense itself as a living being. It must also have the most primitive sensations of taking in nourishment and of what goes with that, even if it takes in nutrition only osmotically, or by unpredictably enfolding with its unformed mass of protoplasm some small food item, digesting it, and expelling the remainder. It must have an unconscious sensation of needing food, and of having had enough. It must be able to assimilate and grow, rather than merely increase quantitatively, as does a crystal or a chemical precipitate. Its body must be in internal correlation, so that its whole metabolism, all its changes of form, every inner and outer motion, and its whole behavior, are regulated. In brief, it must be an individual.

There is also the possibility of a variation in form,

---

[11] The hypothetical production of living organisms directly from inanimate matter.

even if this variation is random, which also presupposes that an inner correlation exists. Even in the simplest kind of reproduction, through division, both parts have an inherited capacity for regeneration. All this presupposes an organic and living apparatus, and therefore an organism, rather than any sort of "almost inorganic" mechanism. The original form sought for by advocates of the theory of descent would, concretely speaking, in all circumstances be a complete organism; it would be the expression of what even at the highest stage of the organic we call "life." We may say, further, that the original form would have be a specialized, adapted living being, even if it were of the most primitive kind, such as some sort of lump of slime without a rigid outline. And even granted all this, we have still not even asked how such a primitive being could subsequently develop over the course of time into a worm, a fish, a mammal, or a human being. Either the capacity for this was already within it in the beginning, and developed with an inner necessity, or it has come about by means of the incredible miracle postulated by natural science—that as a result of accidental external influences over the course of millions of years, this original form has become a mollusc, a crab, and all sorts of other things, in a Darwinian fashion.[12]

Daqué compares the "incredible miracle" of such an original life-form coming into being in the first place (and of the subsequent emergence from it of a mollusc, crab, fish, amphibian, reptile, mammal, ape, and human being in a

[12] Dacqué, *Leben als Symbol* (Munich, 1928), 55ff. VT

Darwinian fashion, by means of accidental external influences) with the more "credible miracle" of the hylozoistic archetype that first distinguished itself from inorganic matter, then put forth the world of plants, then expelled in sequence the various forms of animals, in order at last to appear as the human being of today.

In this view, the human being (or what the human being is some day to become) was the "superman" (*Übermensch*) already present as an efficacious archetype in the original inchoate fire, who, rejecting one unsuitable form after another as too one-sided and specialized, through self-enforced persistence came to be today's human being.

> As the human race excluded more and more bestial elements from itself, its nature became more like the human being of today; this is why the higher animals of the most recent age of earth's history are more like the human beings of the present day than are those of earlier ages [...] It could also be that an as yet undeveloped type of human being might find itself still "developing" precisely by leaving behind—as a more bestial form—what we now are. The "superman" dreamed of thereby acquires natural-historical weight. But the later, complete human being who would be leaving us behind in this way as a lesser type of human being, would not be quantitatively greater than us, but in a certain sense smaller: he would have had to cast off and leave behind, in whole or in part, even *our own* present bestial elements. But he would be *more*, inwardly; he would be a more perfect symbol of the "original form."[13]

---

[13] Ibid., 201. VT. The quotation has been slightly abbreviated.

So, we lay people are faced with two family-trees of the theory of evolution. Both trees are built upon the empirical-phenomenological results of natural science. And we have a choice to make. We have the choice (if we *wish* to choose at all) between the "incredible miracle" of a lump of slime becoming in the course of countless accidents over millions of years an intelligent human person, and the more "credible miracle" of the at least partially conceivable gradual entry upon the stage of the figure of human personhood that had *latently* existed in archetypal form from the very beginning.

The first choice to consider, the "incredible miracle" theory, is that of the transformation (stretched over millions of years) of a lump of slime into human personhood—and this without mother or father, indeed without even an artificer or magician who might know how to conjure such a transformation. Whether this unintended, unguided transformation took place over millions of years or in a quarter of an hour makes no difference as regards its *conceivability*: what is inconceivable remains inconceivable, regardless whether it took place quickly or slowly. In this regard, the biblical account of the creation (even if one takes the "days" of the six-days' labor literally) has the advantage of conceivability in that it presupposes a creating and guiding intelligence at work according to a purposive plan. This allows us to accept the act of creation as *in principle* a conceivable event—by analogy with artistic creation—which we cannot do when it is a question of an uncreated, unborn lump of matter that is said to attain human personhood as a result of being shaken about by accidental external events. Here thinking comes to a halt. Here we must bring blind faith to bear, on the authority of... well, on what authority?

The second choice (the other direction in the theory of evolution) is not a sequel to the atomistic, mechanical materialism harking back to Democritus, but the continuation of the hylozoism of the ancient Ionians and of Aristotle, passed on to us by way of Fechner.[14] This continuation of hylozoism sets before us the archetype of the human being as a cosmic *predisposition* that comes gradually to manifestation. It is "conceivable" in that it displays a certain analogy with what we know of the development of the embryo and growth stages of the human being. For embryonic development is also a metamorphosis from a single fertilized cell to a complete human form. From the very beginning, the embryo develops with an inner necessity rather than as the cumulative result of accidental external influences. In so doing, it exhibits the stages of the unfolding of the human form to its perfection—a form that is indeed invisible but not on that account any less real. Here a human organization, which has been present *in potentia* from the outset, wrestles its way through until it comes to manifestation.

Since the hylozoistic theory of evolution is tied in this

[14] We actually find in physicist Gustav Theodor Fechner (1801–1887) the idea of an archetype which, as Tomberg says in the following sentence, "comes gradually to manifestation." Fechner established that "in its rise from lower stages to that of the human being, the highest being on the planet, nature strives towards spherical form," for which he offers as proof the skull. By studying how animal skulls metamorphose into the human skull, we are able to establish how they seek "to undergo a transformation whereby they strive toward the spherical, and then toward the center of the sphere." Fechner, *Vergleichende Anatomie der Engel* (Leipzig, 1825), 16–17.

respect to an experience, this experience allows the theory to be assimilated in a way that rests on analogy. For one can say to oneself that "the development of the embryo goes through various stages, including some similar in kind to those of an animal, but it is oriented towards the human being right from the beginning; and the human being is, at every one of its stages, the guiding and directing principle." In this way, one can also imagine that the whole of cosmic evolution, or at least the whole of earthly evolution, is a kind of embryonic development that lasts for millions of years rather than for nine months.

This thought can lead to fruitful and valuable results when developed further. Nonetheless, the hylozoistic theory of evolution leaves unanswered the real question regarding the beginning of abiogenesis. For in the case of the human embryo, we know it comes from a father and a mother. But where does the "original form" of the "original matter" carrying the human being within itself as a predisposition come from? From whom, and whence, comes this predisposition? Clearly, we are also dealing with a miracle in the case of the hylozoistic theory of development, a miracle, however, that is partially conceivable and promises indeed to prove fruitful.

⊕

With this we are facing a choice between the theory that the human being is the result of a mechanical, i.e., of an un-thought and un-willed development of material, and the theory that the lower realms of nature (animal, plant, and mineral) are products of the human being as it separates itself from them. If we limit the parameters of the problem, we are left to choose between the thesis that "human beings are descended from the apes" and the thesis that "apes are descended from human beings."[15]

Here, however, it would be appropriate to refer to the fact that even if we have looked into both theories thoroughly and acquired a sufficient overview of the arguments and the factual materials standing behind them, a choice between the two is in the meantime neither necessary nor advisable. After all, these theories are of a metaphysical kind, and as such belong to the great complex of humanity's possible and actual metaphysical theories. Why should we tear these two theories out of the whole complex to which they belong and choose between them before having made sure there is not a third or a fourth theory that might obviate the need to choose between the materialist and the hylozoistic theories of evolution? Ought we not first gather more clues in order to take into consideration the deeper aspects of the problem of the evolution of the world—its philosophical, psychological, historical, and religious aspects? What would be the good of choosing this or that theory of evolution without knowing or understanding the human being as a *human being*, rather than merely as a biological phenomenon? For as an object of *experience*, human beings are not only complicated systems of electrical charges and discharges (as they are for physics), not only prodigiously complicated colonies of cells (as they are for biology), but, beyond these, are also

---

[15] Compare this with the formulation by Rudolf Steiner in a lecture of July, 9, 1924: "You see from this that man did not descend from the apes: man was there, and all the mammals really descended from him, from these human forms in which man remained imperfect. So we must say that the ape descended from man, not that man descended from the ape." https://rsarchive.org/Lectures/19240709p01.html.

thinking beings, moral beings, and creative beings. If we want to understand the "evolution" (or, the coming-into-being) of human beings, and not just that of colonies of cells, we must also understand how our soul and spirit come to be. Moreover, to understand our coming-to-be as human beings, we must take into consideration the *totality* of our coming-into-being—that of our ideals, ideas, concepts, needs, hopes, and abilities, as well as of our bodily organs and our character.

For Hegel, human beings are a stage in the dialectical process of the world-spirit; for biologists, human beings are a stage in the process of the combination and development of cells. But human beings *experience* themselves and are experienced by others neither as they are thought by the world-spirit, nor as a colony of cells. They experience themselves and are experienced by others as *persons* who are neither the world-spirit nor colonies of cells but are themselves *responsible* for their thoughts, words, and deeds—that is, who are free.

Whatever the truth of the matter, it is not the author's intention to confront the reader with the choice between the mechanical-materialist and the hylozoistic theory of evolution, but to illustrate by means of these theories that the *superstructure* of science is not at all scientific, i.e., is not universally valid and binding, but belongs rather to the domain in which quite other criteria than purely scientific ones obtain—namely, the criteria of *personal certainty*. These latter criteria are *not* universally valid and binding; they belong to the domain of the optional, to the domain of freedom. They *can*, however, assist individual human beings, within the inner forum of their own best knowledge and conscience, to attain a degree of certainty matching that of science as an empirical phenomenology and a logical and mathematical method.

Little by little in what follows, the criteria of personal certainty indicated in the previous chapter will be elaborated and illustrated in detail. In this present section, however, it is a question of setting out *one* essential aspect of the "method of personal certainty" by comparing it with methods that claim universal validity and necessity.

One such method (over and above the empirical-phenomenological method already discussed) that claims universal valididy and necessity, is logic (or "symbolic logic," as it is called today, after its amalgamation with mathematics and a more developed version of Kant's transcendental method). Both traditional Aristotelian logic and modern symbolic logic (which is already over a century old) claim universal validity and necessity for their results. Indeed, modern symbolic logic, in particular, which has taken upon itself the mantle of a sort of bloodless inquisition in scientific research, claims to be the "science of science," i.e., the transcendental function of science.

Every logician (Aristotelian, Scholastic, or modern) recognizes that logic has to do with *form*; but it was left to modern logic to develop a science of "pure" logic concerned with *nothing but form*. Even if it had been a central theme for Aristotle himself, there was nevertheless present in his work (and also in the later Aristotelian logic of the Scholastics) an admixture of content-related material in addition to the formal element. Thus, for example, modern logicians maintain that the first principle of traditional logic, that of identity (or "A equals A"), in fact has not only a *formal* sense, but also—to the degree it may signify some particular *content* of a worldview—a *metaphysical* sense. That is, if "A" is imagined as the bearer or subject of attributes, the formula "A equals A" can be interpreted as signifying the persistence of substance even as the features of its appearance change. Modern logic maintains that this interpretation (which also existed historically) implies a metaphysical theory—that of persisting individuality. Aristotle did not himself (as far as we know) formulate the principle of identity in this way, but such a way of interpreting it may indeed be inferred from his well-known formulation that "what is true must in every respect be congruent with itself," i.e., the principle of identity.

However the case might stand with the metaphysical admixture to Aristotelian and Scholastic logic, and however purely formal and worldview-free modern logic might be, traditional and modern logic had and have in mind the same *ideal*: an absolute universality of form, free from any element of the individual and from any element of content. Both the four traditional forms of syllogism (three of which originate with Aristotle, the fourth being ascribed to the celebrated ancient physician Galen) and the five "truth tables" along with the "incomplete sixth truth table" of Rudolf Carnap,[16] are intended to be employed in such a way that the signs of the letters in them may be replaced by any content one likes, while they are themselves perfectly free of content, i.e., *formal*.

What distinguishes modern logic from traditional logic is that the latter accepts grammatical form as a signpost to log-

[16] Cf. Rudolf Carnap, *Introduction to Symbolic Logic and Its Applications* (New York: Dover Publications, 1958), 10–13. VT

ical form and thereby constitutes an instrument adequate to the needs of the philosopher, who makes use of the means of *language*. Modern logic, however, wishes to be a language in itself logical and *nothing but* logical—a language, moreover, that makes it possible to express *all* logically relevant elements (e.g., relations for which there is no formal means of expression in traditional logic, and which are expressed in that logic using words drawn from ordinary language), as well as excluding *all* logically irrelevant elements.

If "mathematizing philosophers" such as Leibniz once worked on traditional logic, modern logic is the fruit of work on logic by "philosophizing mathematicians" such as Gottlob Frege, Alfred North Whitehead, and Bertrand Russell. Modern logic is the result of work on the foundations of mathematics, logic, and philosophy; it is the epistemology of these disciplines. This result is the amalgamation of three fields into a fourth, that of modern logic.

> The reason for this lies in the historical fact that, during the past century, mathematicians became increasingly more aware of the need to examine again, and to reconstruct, the foundations of the whole edifice of mathematics.[17]

Thus, systems were worked out that were supposed to provide the foundation for a reconstruction of mathematics (arithmetic, analysis, function theory, the calculus of infinitesimals). The systems of Frege, Whitehead and Russell, and Hilbert have shown their aptitude for this task; and on this basis there occurred the amalgamation of logic and mathematics. Thus, Gottlob Frege says, in concluding his *Die Grundlagen der Arithmetik*, that he hopes, in his work:

[17] Ibid., 3. VT

to have made it probable that arithmetical laws are
analytic judgments and are therefore *a priori*. Accordingly, arithmetic is only a more extensively developed
logic, and each arithmetical proposition is a logical
law, but one which has been arrived at by deduction.
The applications of arithmetic to the explanation of
nature would, then, be logical reworkings of
observed facts;[18] calculations would be inferences.
[The laws of number] are applicable to valid judgments about things in the external world: they are
laws of the laws of nature. They do not assert any
connection between natural appearances, but rather a
connection between judgments; and among these
judgments are the laws of nature.[19]

Frege declares that arithmetic is "a more extensively developed logic," that its laws of number are "laws of the laws of
nature," and that herein lies the essence of modern logic's
concern, as well as its claim. But as it happens, neither its
concern nor its claim is limited to equating mathematics
with logic: they go further. Modern logic also wishes to be
the direct successor and continuator of Kant's "Copernican
discovery": his transcendental method.

⊕

Whereas Kant established his categories of pure reason on
the ground of introspection (i.e., by observing the unfolding of his own thoughts), modern logic wishes to know and
to set out the categorial structure of knowledge, not by

---

[18] The act of observing already includes a logical component. VT
[19] Gottlob Frege, *Die Grundlagen der Arithmetik* (Breslau, 1884), §87.
VT

means of introspection (which it finds too subjective), but by investigating the logical and methodological content of scientific results. In this, modern logic starts out from the view that the successful achievements of science represent *objectified* human reason, and thereby make possible a more objective application of the transcendental method of "thinking about thinking" than that of introspection. Modern logic wishes, so to speak, to draw inferences "from the fruit to the tree" by examining the achievements of science (in particular its successful theories) from the point of view of the categorial structure of reason expressed in these theories.

Since, however, Kant demonstrated that a metaphysics going beyond the categorial structure of reason is not possible (i.e., that transcendental logic is the only form of metaphysics possible on the basis of pure reason), and since for his part Hegel converted transcendental logic into a metaphysics (by declaring the categorial structure of reason to be identical with the structure of the world), modern logic makes the claim to be a modern, rational metaphysics, with the result that modern logic is on the one hand the foundation of mathematics, logic, and metaphysics, and on the other the mathematical and logical sign language for these fields.

However far the concerns and claims of modern logic may extend, it remains a question of the ideal of logic and of the so-called exact sciences as such, which is to say of the ideal of universal validity and necessity (i.e., of results that are supposed to be completely free from psychological and empirical contingencies). It is the ideal of purely formal cognition, of pure form. When all is said and done, traditional logic had in mind (though perhaps not so self-consciously as does modern logic) an *ars magna* similar to that of Ramon Llull—that is, a *mechanical* procedure for discovering the necessary argument, and for drawing the necessary conclusions. In this sense, the "calculus of statements" of modern logic, whose value is supposed to lie in the fact

> that the rules about combinations of statements are set out in it with a completeness appropriate to the needs of science, and are brought together in a system free from contradictions,[20]

is to be seen as a further step in the direction of the mechanization of the process of thinking.

The working out of a system such as makes possible a calculus of statements requires a very great labor of thinking. Once this work has been carried out, however, it need never be repeated, because thereafter we will be able to apply its results in a mechanical way, just as we do the formulas of arithmetic (algebra) that had at one time to be thought through, but now lie ready to hand to solve problems. Even Frege admits that it is possible "by means of real thinking" to develop "mathematical sign language so extensively that it, as they say, thinks for you."[21]

In the end, the task and goal of modern logic is to be able to replace the hard work of "actual thinking" with a system of tables (rather like logarithmic tables) in a calculus of statements. But even traditional logic, with its four forms of categorical syllogism, sought the greatest possible economy of thought; by means of its results, it meant to save as

---

[20] In his work *Ars magna, generalis et ultima*, Ramon Llull (1232–1316) claimed to be able to acquire new knowledge by means of an apparatus capable of mechanically combining concepts.

[21] Frege, ibid., iv. VT

much of the labor of thinking as possible and to make forming judgments as effortless as possible.

⊕

Since the goal both of traditional and of modern logic consists in providing those engaged in scientific pursuits with a sort of ready apparatus that "will think for them" (i.e., that renders service in the field of formal thinking), we need not take an example expressed in the mathematical sign language of formal logic to illustrate the difference between the *material* knowledge of personal certainty and *formal* logical knowledge: for this, a simple example from traditional logic will suffice.

Let us take the proposition "All men are mortal; Socrates is a man; therefore, Socrates is mortal." Here we have a logically correct judgment that is formally unimpeachable. But the first part of the proposition (the premise) is no mere result of logic but of *experience*. Experience has taught us that human beings are mortal. This experience consists in the fact that after a certain period of time the phenomenon we call a "human being" disappears from the experiential realm of our external senses, even if that human being may live on for a long time in the realm of our internal sense (i.e., psychologically as a recollection, an imagined form, a dream form, a shape of feeling, a shape of the will, etc.).

Such disappearances of individual human beings from the realm of external sensory perception recurred so many times that the experiential (i.e., inductive) conclusion was drawn that all men are mortal. Note, however, that this "logically possible" conclusion was drawn solely on the basis of a higher or lower degree of probability. Since such a conclusion is, *logically*, only a question of something probable (even if its degree of probability is very high), the opening premise should really read "if all men are mortal."

Now, since the middle term of the syllogism, "Socrates is a man," is likewise a statement of experience, it also is neither demonstrable nor refutable by means of logic, and should really read "if Socrates is a man." Thus amended, the whole syllogism should read: "If all men are mortal, and if Socrates is a man, it follows that Socrates is mortal also." In this formulation, it is solely a question of the logical connection between the three judgments, not of their content. This is clear if we consider that, logically, the opposite would be just as correct if the kind of connection (the inferential *form*) remained unaltered. That is, we could equally well say: "If all men are immortal, and if Socrates is a man, it follows that Socrates is immortal also." The decision as to whether the first or the second proposition is *true* (recalling that both are logically *correct*) is solely a question of their material or substantive *truth*; and to establish such truth, a third criterion must be invoked: *experience*. In other words, *certainty* in the matter of whether Socrates is mortal or immortal is to be sought elsewhere than in the field of logic. It is not to be sought in the field of *formal* logic, but in that of *material* knowledge.

Non-specialists unconcerned with promoting a specialized field of science or developing a method peculiar to this field, but concerned instead with personal certainty in questions about life, may of course gratefully make use of formal logic as a means of learning to think with precision, care, and logical consistency. But they will not expect from it any conclusions about *their own* concern for personal certainty. This is because, even if traditional or modern logic were to give a positive answer to such questions about life, this answer would not satisfy them, owing to its merely formal character: the answer given would have come about on the basis of nothing more than a combination of things being brought into systematic order, whereas what *matters* to them is the way things actually are and the wisdom that ordered them in just this way. The answer from the side of formal logic would be too shallow, too superficial, to motivate them to order their lives according to its conclusions.

The Christian martyrs possessed a degree of personal certainty so strong that even the threat of a painful death could not shake it. But they did not owe their personal certainty to the insight that God and His Incarnation are logical necessities. They owed it, rather, to a process of the *becoming* and the *ripening* of their total being. We catch a glimpse of what this means in Augustine's *Confessions*, or even in that fine modern testament to human becoming, Karl Stern's *The Pillar of Fire*.[22]

Personal certainty, which cannot be acquired by means of logical syllogisms or the implications of modern logic, but is suffered for, longed for, striven for—which grows and ripens—is the fruit of a transformation of our total consciousness. It rests upon acquiring the dimension of depth, a dimension that plays no role whatsoever in formally logi-

---

[22] Karl Stern (1906–1975) was a German psychiatrist who emigrated to Canada, where in 1943 he converted from Judaism to Catholicism. In his autobiographical *The Pillar of Fire* (NY: Harcourt, Brace, and Company, 1951), 229, he wrote: "If it were true, I used to think, that God had become man, and that His life and death had a personal meaning to every single person among all those millions of existences spent in the stench of slums, in a horizonless world, in the suffocating anguish of enmities, sickness, and dying—if that were true, it would be something tremendously worth living for."

cal judgment. It is depth alone that fosters the growth of personal certainty, and determines its degree. The Christian martyrs were people of depth, and out of this depth they created a power of certainty, or of faith, which there was no way of breaking.

⊕

But we must ask: is formal logic the only kind of thinking capable of truth? Is it the only possible method by which thinking can distinguish true from false and ascertain the true? Does all clear, certain, and logically consistent thinking absolutely *have* to be formally logical? Is formal logic the only means by which thinking can become privy to the truth and overcome deception? For those disposed to cast their gaze over the larger picture of the spiritual history of humanity, the doubt just formulated cannot so easily be dispensed with on objective grounds, let alone for deeper reasons. What quite naturally comes to mind in entering upon this question are such stars of the first magnitude in this domain as Kant, Plato, and Aristotle.

Kant. As for Kant, although he made one of the greatest contributions to formal logic, he did not arrive at certainty about God, immortality, and freedom by employing it; he did so by way of the moral or material logic he described as "pure practical reason." In Kant we confront the fact that a celebrated thinker and acute logician attained personal certainty about the existence of God, immortality, and freedom neither on the basis of external authority nor by means of formal logic, but by creating that certainty out of the nature of moral consciousness—or at least out of *his* moral consciousness. And indeed, this is just how he created it: not as a mystic of feeling but as a *thinker* making use of a logic *not* resting upon the laws or the categorial structure of theoretical reason, but upon the categorial structure of *moral* consciousness. Kant's certainty regarding the existence of God, freedom, and immortality is an achievement of *moral logic*. The formal logic of pure reason could not deliver it. For Kant, where a logic grounded upon the principle of *necessity* was obliged to concede defeat, a logic grounded upon the principle of *freedom* (= moral consciousness) was crowned with success. Let us listen to what he himself has to say about it:

> So, the reason why the attempt to prove the existence of God and immortality by purely theoretical means has failed is that no knowledge of the supersensible is at all possible by this means (that of concepts of nature). The reason why the moral approach (by way of the concept of freedom) has, conversely, succeeded, is that here the supersensible element that forms the basis—freedom—not only supplies material for the knowledge of the other supersensible element (of the final moral purpose and the conditions of its practicability) through a particular law of causality that originates in freedom, but also demonstrates its reality as a fact by means of actions. For just this reason, the only ground of proof it can give is that which is valid from a practical point of view—which is also the only one that religion needs.
>
> In this connection, it remains very remarkable that, of the three ideas of reason—*God, freedom,* and *immortality*—freedom is the only concept of the supersensible that gives proof (by means of the causality which we think in it) of its objective reality in nature. This occurs through the effect that freedom

itself is able to bring about in nature. Just by this means, it makes it possible to connect the other two with nature, but also to connect all three into a religion. Moreover, it shows that we have a principle within us that is able to specify the idea of the supersensible in us—and therefore also the idea of the supersensible outside us—so that it becomes a cognition, even if that cognition is only possible from a practical point of view. . . .[23]

In this context we should note that vanishingly little has been done towards the further development of moral logic as compared with what has been done for formal logic. And yet, moral logic is something that by its nature is extremely promising and therefore worthy of further development. We cannot overlook the possibility that Kant's "morally sufficient ground" for the reality of God, immortality, and freedom might be a seed out of which much else could grow, or that moral logic might perhaps harbor within itself limitless possibilities of development.

We should not suppose that the possibilities of "moral logic," as the logic of practical reason, are limited simply because they pertain to practical purposes. For where are the limits of practice? Should "practice" be limited to external actions alone? Should it be limited to the realm of doing and of letting be? Are not utterances actions? Is silence not a letting be? Is therapeutic care for the spiritual health of humanity and its culture not a matter of practical reason? Is the duty to seek the truth and to help it triumph over illusions and lies not a matter of practical reason? Everything

[23] Immanuel Kant, *Kritik der Urteilskraft*. Zweiter Teil: Kritik der teleologischen Urteilskraft. 6 Aufl. (Leipzig 1924), B 466–67. VT

with a moral significance, everything morally exacting or dangerous, belongs to the realm of practical reason, to the realm of moral logic. There is nothing in the world too small to have a moral significance in some context or other. There is also nothing in the world too large to retain a moral significance. Practical reason (moral logic) has the whole world for its object, just like theoretical reason and formal logic. What differs in each case is only the *relationship* to the world: that is, whether we wish to consider the world from a *moral* or from a *mechanical* point of view.

The sun, the moon, and the stars can be considered masses of matter within the mechanically moving system of gravitational relationships. But they can also be considered the revelation of a prevailing *order* of the highest possible moral and practical significance. For it is within this prevailing order that we have to carry out our actions and set our goals. How would it be if the sun rose in the East today, tomorrow in the West, and the day after not at all? *Reliability* in the world is a moral and practical factor in human life that is of no less moral and practical significance than the reliability of the people to whom we are joined in friendship, marriage, and work. What kind of friend would someone be if they could not be relied upon? If we could not rely upon the world, what kind of world would it be?

All things can be considered either from a mechanical or a moral standpoint. Formal logic is the law of the mechanical view of things; moral logic is the law of the moral view of things. Practical reason is not restricted in its object to those human actions and goals lying closest to hand; its object extends as far as the moral concerns of all humanity extend. And, in principle, there are no limits to how far the latter can extend.

91

Plato. As for Plato, he does not owe his conviction that the world is a work of art (i.e., that it is the expression of archetypes or ideas) to formal logic either. He *experienced* the knowledge to which he owed this conviction, and he described that experience as a kind of birth out of the depths of the unconscious or the supra-conscious. He also compared it to the process of recollection, in which something not present to consciousness, something "forgotten," surfaces from the depths of the unconscious or of the supra-conscious. Now, neither "birth" nor "recollection" are canons of formal logic; they are, instead, *creative* events. We may believe this or not, but Plato's thought was, *for him*, a creation out of the depths. The same was true for his teacher Socrates, in whose name Plato always spoke.

If Plato was not making use of formal logic, might he have been making use of what Kant, millennia later, described as "pure practical reason," or moral logic? For "logic" (i.e., an ordered thinking) is certainly characteristic of Plato. He was, after all, a *thinker*, not an emotive mystic. If we observe Plato's intellectual world more closely, we can establish two things: he made extensive use of both formal and moral logic in the exposition and grounding of particular parts of his doctrinal edifice. But taken as a whole, this edifice is actually the result of a *third* kind of thinking, a third logic, namely, the *logic of artistic creation*.

If we understand by "logic" the law-likeness that rules in the "meaningful word" (*logos*), then each essentially distinct area of meaning of the "meaningful word" must have its own "logic." The ideal of *harmony* lying at the basis of artistic endeavor (the ideal of bringing the "how" into agreement with the "what") brings with it a "logic" also, just as the ideal of universal validity (universal truth) brings with it a "logic," namely, formal logic. If, however, it is a matter only of the "what," then we are in the realm of moral logic.

The creative act embraces the archetype of the "what" that is to be created; it embraces what is created; and it embraces the process whereby what is to be created comes into being. This is the foundation of the logic of artistic creation. These are its basic elements, just as subject, predicate, and attribute are the basic elements of traditional formal logic. For Plato, the world was "what had been created": a work of art. He called the archetypes of this created world "ideas," and he thought of the coming-into-being of this world as a process analogous to that of artistic creation, which is to say *the transformation of the ideal into the real* that takes place when a work of art comes into being. Plato's demiurge is really the world-artist, who brings the ideas into outer appearance.

Is an artistic or aesthetic logic conceivable? Why should it not be, especially since Plato made full use of it? And after all, Kant devoted to it one of his three most important works, the *Critique of the Power of Judgment*, in which he described this logic precisely as "the power of aesthetic judgment"! Even if an untruth most often seems distasteful and morally inferior, why, merely on that account, should we deny to taste and to the moral sense the same value as criteria of judgment as has been accorded the sense of truth? In other words, if a thing has its correctness and its truth, why should it not also have its perfection of expression and its moral significance? If the world is a law-like order, why should it not at the same time also be a *kosmos*, i.e., a great work of art? Or for that matter, why should it not be the scene upon which freedom (i.e., the moral life) is to be realized?

Just as moral logic is not only conceivable alongside formal logic, but in fact exists, so aesthetic logic is not only conceivable alongside formal logic, but in fact also exists. Regarding this, Kant says:

> There are three kinds of antinomy because there are three powers of knowledge—understanding, the power of judgment, and reason—of which each (as a higher power of knowledge) must have its own *a priori* principles.[24]

Now, if each of the three powers "must have its own *a priori* principles of consciousness" then each must have its own *logic*, since logic is nothing other than the use of the *a priori* principles of consciousness. Logic is the *inner* law-likeness of consciousness. It is the enduring structure of consciousness. And just as there is such a structure of theoretical thinking, so there is also a structure of aesthetic thinking and of moral thinking.

Where these three "logics" are concerned, however, it is not a matter of three separate worlds or of three separate structures of consciousness, but of three aspects of *one* world and of three structures or organs of *one* consciousness. The true, the beautiful, and the good make up the *tri-une* character of human spiritual life, and all *real* achievements of this spiritual life have the quality that in them these three aspects are in harmony. This harmony is perfectly free from compulsion and *makes no claim to universal validity*: it is the free concern of each individual person to seek it and to find it. There is no universally valid

---

[24] *Kritik der ästhetischen Urteilskraft*, B 243–44. VT

and binding "science" of this harmony, nor can there be such a science.

If the several billion inhabitants of the earth should have arrived at the insight that personal certainty consists in the harmony of the results achieved in these three ways (i.e., should they all have become, consciously or unconsciously, believers in the Holy Trinity), it might be said that this point of view would have risen to the status of "universal validity"; but all the same, it would still not be "universally valid."[25] For its universal validity would be the result of the many billion particular events of personal insight and personal growth, and by no means the result of the alleged binding necessity of some impersonal method whose claim to being universally valid has been purchased at the cost of jettisoning what is actually particular and personal, leaving behind some fabricated "universal residue" thereof.

Personal certainty presupposes personhood and freedom, which means to say the complete absence of compulsion, even that of theoretical "proof." Personal certainty is not a *science*; rather, it is, quite precisely, *certainty*.[26] Certainty is not compelled by "proof." Certainty is born upon, and grows upon, the ground of freedom.

[25] The distinction is between *allgemeine Geltung* and *allgemeingültig*.
[26] Here the distinction is between *Wissenschaft* and *Gewissheit*.

IV

Uncompelled Knowledge:
System, Order, Symbolism

ONCEPTS STRICTLY LIMITED TO A SINGLE MEAN-
ING, arrayed in a system free of gaps or contradictions, constitute the goal, indeed the ideal,
not only of the exact sciences, but also of the so-
called humanistic sciences such as theology, philosophy, and
jurisprudence. Most often, theologians, philosophers, and
jurists have in mind the ideal of the same sort of system as
do physicists, mathematicians, and logicians. Striving for
monovalence and systematicity sometimes goes so far that
knowledge (as sharply defined) and *truth* (as the systemiza-
tion of that sharply-defined knowledge) are equated with
each other. In the end, the claim made by the humanistic
sciences to scientificity comes down to their sharing with
the exact sciences the goal of attaining, with the help of
clear and distinct concepts, a closed, comprehensive system
without gaps or contradictions. The humanistic sciences
lack empirical proofs of predictability, but in their case this
is replaced by coherence: by the way individual elements of
the system mutually reinforce and support each other, and
by the absence of internal contradictions.

Hegel, for example, ascribed to "system" a significance
equivalent to "knowledge of truth." For him, systematic

97

thinking and knowledge of truth were one and the same thing. He considered the systematic development of the concepts "being," "non-being," and "becoming"—as thesis, antithesis, and synthesis—to be both necessary and sufficient to know the world and its whole past and future, i.e., to be able to look at the world intellectually as a system free of gaps or contradictions.

The same is true of Marxism, which took over Hegel's dialectical method. Marxists know all about the world and world history, its whither and whence. Admittedly, they do not know all the facts, and yet (to their satisfaction) they know all the laws of what takes place in the world. They conjure for themselves the conviction that they do really know these laws, that they are the true laws of what happens in the world, and that this lawful system of theirs is free from any gaps or contradictions. For Marxists, their system and truth are one and the same thing.

⊕

In what, then, does the essence of the "monovalent" concept (the concept strictly limited to a single meaning) and of the "system" consist? Let us take as an example the concept of freedom and consider its meaning in different contexts. In international law, for example, one speaks of the "freedom of the seas," meaning that beyond the boundaries of the so-called territorial waters[1] the ocean is open to the ships of any nation. The ocean does not belong to any state, and the freedom of the sea thus means "free use" of it by

---

[1] Hugo Grotius (1583–1645) devoted a treatise to this problem: *Mare liberum*, Leiden, 1605. VT

states, particularly for the purposes of navigation and fishing. Then again, when we speak in ordinary usage of the freedom of persons or citizens, we do *not* mean the "free use" of persons or of citizens by a third party. On the contrary, we mean that the person or the citizen alone disposes over himself. To free a slave means to dispense with the right to dispose over him, and to hand this right over to the former slave himself. But when we speak of our "free will," we mean neither that our will is at everyone else's disposal (as the ocean is at the disposal of states for their use) nor that the will disposes over itself, since the will can just as little dispose over itself as Baron von Munchausen can pull himself up into the air by his pigtails. What we mean by our free will is the capacity to *choose* between objects, actions, good and evil, etc.

The concept of freedom is given a different content in Hegel's work. By "freedom" Hegel understands not the will's capacity to choose, but the will's obedience to reason. For Hegel, being free does not mean doing what one wants; it means wanting, and doing, what reason commands. The concept of "freedom" has still another meaning in Schiller's work. For Schiller, freedom means a state of consciousness in which the irrational play-instinct and the strict command of reason are united in the experience of the beautiful, and that these contract an alliance for the sake of the beautiful. Then both the mind's control of instinct and instinct's control of the mind come to an end: we are *free*.

The concept of "freedom" has yet another content in Indian religious philosophy, in the *Vedanta* and *Yoga*. There, freedom means the state of having been freed from the bonds that tie consciousness to *maya* (the illusion of separate existence in the world of appearances). Here the content of the concept of "freedom" is the repose of a consciousness that is without desires.

If we turn to the New Testament, to the epistles of the apostle Paul, we meet another concept of freedom, distinct from those just introduced. "Freedom in Christ," which is there contrasted with "unfreedom under the law," is the freedom from fear and doubt in life and in death. Death's "sting" has been removed, as well as the reason for fear and doubt. For the human being's task will henceforth no longer be completed out of fear of punishment, but out of love. The content of the Pauline concept of freedom is love of God and humanity.

Finally, Nikolai Berdyaev, who continued work begun in Jakob Boehme's and Schelling's thinking about freedom, gave the concept of freedom the content of "creation out of nothing." For him, freedom means the capacity to bring forth being from non-being.

⊕

In order, then, to obtain a strictly limited or monovalent concept of freedom, we will have to choose one particular concept from among those introduced above (or from among other concepts of freedom not discussed here), or else seek an all-embracing concept that contains all these concepts and is to be obtained by abstracting from them.

The first way is easy, and incurs no greater difficulty than satisfying our conscience as to whether we may simply hold our *own* personal conception of freedom to be *the* concept of freedom. As far as the second way is concerned (the attempt to define a clear and distinct concept of freedom that would embrace all existing conceptions of freedom), it is extremely difficult to find some one definition that would simultaneously and equitably do justice to such varied conceptions as those put forward by Berdyaev, the apostle Paul, Patañjali (*Yoga*), Hegel, theology, and jurisprudence! Should we nevertheless surmount this difficulty and recover our peace of mind by means of some sort of definition (such as "freedom is a being's unrestricted and uncoerced development" or "freedom is the capacity for uncaused causation" or "freedom is the state of the subject in which it legislates for itself"), we would still have to deal with the question of what is actually *gained* by such a definition. Certainly, we would acquire thereby a clear-cut concept bringing together the different aspects of the concept of freedom under a single heading, but this will have been achieved at the expense of the *comprehensiveness* of the concept of freedom. For such an all-embracing concept or definition of freedom could only be a "remainder" left after *stripping away* the individual particularities of the various concepts of freedom. What is common to all (or to many) of the conceptions of freedom will have been found and defined, but at the price of having lost what is particular to each of them singly. Conversely, however, if we concentrate solely on the particular, we lose what is held in common. How, then, might we express the concept of freedom so as to do justice both to what is common to all the possible ideas of it, and to what is particular to each of those ideas?

Since the very earliest times, and in every part of the world, human consciousness has found an answer to this question in the *symbol.* The symbol is intended to be a means of expression that has a single meaning as well as a multiplicity of meanings. In the symbol, what is held in common and what is particular abide together; they are combined, not in a definition, but in an *emblem.* If, rather than bringing the various conceptions of freedom together under the single heading of an all-embracing definition, we combine them in the emblem of a central point from which rays emanate to the periphery, we acquire a form of expression that can contain many monovalent concepts, and yet bring them all into a unity. A symbol never collapses, no matter how many distinctly different concepts we might want to create out of it. Neither does a symbol ever wither away into a mere abstraction, no matter how far we might progress in seeking and finding its final and ultimate content. The *cross* placed above churches, and inside them, means a great many things; and yet, in these many things, it means only one thing. It is a true symbol.

⊕

Let us return to our examination of concepts strictly limited to a single meaning, and the systems made up of them. Why do we want clear-cut concepts in the first place? Why do we take such pains to strip from language (and likewise from the language of thinking) its capacity to stimulate and its power of suggestion, and to turn it into an instrument of exact communication, of signaling strictly determined by conventions? The answer seems ready to hand. We strive for singularity of meaning as a way to avoid a multiplicity of meanings, so that we may better understand each other using words and concepts in such a way that no misunderstandings can arise through their use. The aim of the search for singularity of meaning is *to obviate misunderstanding*.

Let us allow this explanation to stand for now, and ask further: *About what* ought we to be able to understand each other without any possibility of misunderstanding? About everything in our hearts, about everything we are thinking—thus goes the simplest answer. But is it *really* a matter of what is in *our* hearts, of what *we* human beings are thinking? To answer this, let us imagine that we have attained the ideal of monovalent meaning. This would mean that as individual human beings, as persons, we can only say what is made possible and what is permitted by a universal agreement regarding the valid contents of language and of concepts—and nothing more. A language made monovalent by means of convention will indeed be an excellent instrument for communicating and understanding what "one" thinks, but not for communicating what *I* think or what *you* think. Such a language made monovalent by means of convention will not be an adequate means of expression for what any *given* person may have on his or her mind, or in his or her heart. This follows from the fact that the requirement for universally valid monovalence or singularity of meaning brings with it the requirement that anything individual, anything someone may have on their mind or in their heart, should be silenced. In other words, absolutely clear and distinct language necessarily excludes and silences the human being as a *person*. "One" will indeed be able to utter quite precisely all "one" is thinking, but *you* and *I* will be condemned to silence. For *you* and *I* will no longer have a language at our disposal.

Real interaction and exchange of thoughts among human beings consists of a series of events that include a great deal more than the mere exchange of words as sound signals. All words are *stimuli* much more than they are communications in the sense of a news report. If two people interact in words or in writing, their interaction takes place not only at the level of transmitting words (the level of receiving word-transmissions and interpreting them with waking consciousness), but simultaneously at the deeper, "sleeping" levels of consciousness. If this were not the case, if we relied solely on our technical ability to interpret words, quick and direct understanding between people would be completely impossible. Why so? Because managing to understand anything anyone said would have to be preceded by a protracted debate regarding every word employed in the conversation, and about every concept communicated by those words.

Usually this is not necessary. For the most part, we manage to understand each other with the help of a few suggestions because we are not only listening with our ears but are also paying attention with our feelings and our hearts; and when we speak, we do so not only with our tongues but also with the powers of communication vested in our ability to think, in our emotional lives, in everything pulsing within us. A conversation is the creation of a circular path of pulsations between people. Any other sort of "conversation" can only be hot air or argument.

Interaction between people is an exchange of communicative effects of *many different* kinds, all happening at the same time. It carries within itself elements belonging to the realm beyond waking consciousness. If there were no such elements, *music* would be impossible. What would a "clear and distinct communication" of playing the violin to a listener be like, and what would that listener "experience" as a result of such a performance? There are, however, many kinds of music. That of musical instruments is not the only one. There is also a kind of music that accompanies conversation. It is this music that makes it possible for conversation to arrive at an understanding that surpasses words and their literal content.

The stirrings of the deeper layers of consciousness that accompany human speech are a particular kind of music. It is a music that fills the space between the words (and even between the individual concepts) with significance. This *accompaniment* to the words spoken is as essential to our ability to understand each other with words as is the spoken or written word itself: it is in truth the element in which individual persons understand each other. And the more individual a person is, the stronger and more perceptible is the music "accompanying" that person's speech. The gospel vividly suggests this when it says of Jesus's instructing the people, that "unlike their own teachers, he taught with a note of authority." (Matt 7:29) This tells us first and foremost that Jesus's speech was accompanied by so much arresting and revelatory "music" that, by comparison, the speech of the Pharisees and biblical scholars seemed empty and ineffective.

If we wish to experience in its purity and strength the harmony of clear speech and the music accompanying it, we can do no better than to take the speeches (as given in John's gospel) in which the Master bids farewell to his disciples, and to let them have their effect upon us—not interpreting these speeches, nor forcing them, but simply allowing them to have their effect, just as we let music have its effect on us:

> If you love me, you will obey my commands; and I
> will ask the Father, and he will give you another to be
> your Advocate, who will be with you for ever—the
> Spirit of truth. The world cannot receive him,

because the world neither sees nor knows him; but
you know him, because he dwells with you and is in
you. I will not leave you bereft; I am coming back to
you. In a little while the world will see me no longer,
but you will see me; because I live, you too will live;
then you will know that I am in my Father, and you in
me and I in you. The man who has received my commands and obeys them—he it is who loves me; and
he who loves me will be loved by my Father; and I
will love him and disclose myself to him.

(John 14:16–21)

Is it possible not to perceive the music of this farewell
speech, a music like that of the sunset? Who, with even a
little heart left, or ears even half open, can escape the deeply
magical effect of these words? How plain the words are,
how genuine the speech, how shoreless the bright ocean of
the world's deepest secrets revealed in it! We read, we hearken, we become still and bright; the stillness and the brightness grow, we are gripped by them; and we know that the
world is vast, that being is an incomprehensible, precious
gift, that life is infinitely valuable. If there was *one* being
who spoke like this, if only *one* being was able to fashion
words like these… then *all* beings are sanctified.

The language of concepts and words strictly limited to a
single meaning lies open to dissection. The language in
which individual persons interact with each other, on the
other hand, lies open to stimulus, suggestion, and spiritual
transfusion: the farewell speeches in John's gospel are a
blood transfusion.

⊕

Systems. Let us return to the question: "Why do we want

concepts limited to a single meaning in the first place?" The answer that now presents itself for discussion is that we want them for the sake of a *system*. If we have before our eyes the ideal of an all-embracing system that is free from gaps and contradictions, we cannot help but try to ensure that none of the elements of the system (the individual concepts, and, indeed, even the factual material) display their *own* content and value, but receive instead a content and value corresponding to the highest principles of the system in question.

Thus the concept of freedom receives a completely different content and value within the Marxist system than it does within a system of liberal political thought. The principle determining the content and value of the concept of freedom in the Marxist system is the power wielded by one social class (the proletariat) over the economy, whereas in a liberal system the content and value of the concept of freedom is determined by the principle of the greatest possible scope being given to the individual person. One system orients all its concepts towards the central principle of economy and class, or class economy; the other orients all its concepts towards the central principle of the free initiative of individual persons, or personal initiative. The influence these systems exercise over individual concepts can be pictured as a center (representing the ruling principle of the system) towards which, as regards their content and value, the individual concepts point.

Thus, in Freud's system of psychology, the pleasure principle determines not only the content and value of all the concepts belonging directly to the system, but also the content and value of all the concepts that come into contact with it in *any* way. This is how sexual satisfaction and mystical union with God come to signify, essentially, two ways of yielding to the same pleasurable satisfaction, in which all that differs are the "channels" through which this pleasure flows. Religion, metaphysics, and art are reduced in this way to various ways of living out the "libido," i.e., to forms of gratified desire. Those under the sway of this system invoke the pleasure principle as a kind of "philosophers' stone": just as the alchemical philosophers' stone turns everything it touches into gold, so does the pleasure principle turn everything it touches into gratified desire.

It would be unjust, however, to ascribe such miraculous powers as these solely to the highest principle of the *Freudian* system, for *all* systems display the tendency not only to attribute to their own most fundamental concepts the content and value required by the highest principle of their own system but also to project this content and value onto any and all concepts with which they come into contact. All systems have at their center only certain particular ruling principles, which usually become "philosophers' stones" that turn everything they touch into the "gold" of the given system.

Systems, like political states, tend always to expand into and conquer new territories. They are essentially expansionist. Thus Freud's teaching leads everything back to pleasure and unpleasure, Marxism to class struggle over economic goods, utilitarianism to utility, and so on. They are all in possession of a particular philosophers' stone, which they staunchly set about bringing to bear on all things.

But again, why in the first place do people strive for an all-embracing system that is free of gaps or contradictions? Where does the fascinating, even hypnotizing, effect of systems come from?

⊕

Power and Force. Power and force[2] are essentially distinct. We can be forceful without having any power. Inversely, we can be weak and yet have great power at our disposal. When we engage in physical gymnastics, concentration practices, and any other exercises we may choose to undertake, we develop our *forces* and increase our performance *capacities*. Machines on the other hand, which "stand in" for our *incapacities*, signify *power*. If I can play a piece of music on the piano, this is a capacity of mine, my *skill* (*Kraft*); but if I set my phonograph to playing a record, this is not an expression of my force or skill, but of my *power* (*Macht*). To strive for force or skill is to strive for the capacity *to do something*; to strive for power is to strive to *have something done for us that we ourselves cannot do.*

All machines and mechanisms are stand-ins for force or skill. They make it possible to perform something that we lack the capacity to do on our own. For this reason, every mechanism is an expression of a striving for power. But then, what is the ideal of a perfect system of thought other than a "mechanism" that (once constructed) is supposed to enable achievements in thinking that likewise exceed our unassisted capacity to perform? Have we not all experienced, either personally or through others, how *easy* it is to answer questions and to account for phenomena if we have a system (whether whole or partial) at our fingertips; and inversely, how *difficult* it is to find an answer starting out from the nub of an individual situation, or from the heart of the matter, rather than by appealing to a system? We

---

[2] *Macht und Kraft.*

need only recall how *little* in the first case our force, our skill, is called upon, and how *much*, in the second case, it is needed.

Take Marxists: they can answer any given question in the twinkling of an eye. At least, they can do so to their *own* satisfaction. God? An invention of the exploiting class for the purpose of distracting the exploited classes from the fact of their exploitation. Religion? A superstructure fabricated by the exploiting class for the purpose of fixing the attention of the exploited classes upon "God" rather than upon their rights. Science? The instrument by which the currently ruling class exercises power over nature and other people. Etc. For Marxists, it is child's play to answer any question whatever. This is because they have ready to hand a mechanical apparatus, a *system*, that takes on the greater part of the labor of answering questions. *The system does the work for them.* Systems are so attractive and fascinating because they do most of the thinking for people—thereby increasing, not their skill, but their power.

⊕

Order. At this juncture it is important to point out that a *system* should not be mistaken for an *order.* The results of ordered thinking represent something essentially different from the result of systematic thinking. Whereas thinking under the rubric of a system is built around a single ruling principle, thinking in accordance with order (i.e., ordered thinking) takes into account many principles at the same time, while still retaining its quality of order. This ordering quality may become evident in how issues set before it for consideration follow from one from another in an orderly way according to their actual content; or, even more evidently, they may manifest as stages of *growth*, as from a seed—that is, as making explicit what was first implicit.

Clearly, the *Summa Theologiae of* St Thomas Aquinas does not present a system, but an order. The many *quaestiones* St Thomas poses are answered in ordered succession solely according to their actual content. He does not "answer" the *quaestiones* he raises by the expedient of invoking the aid of some single principle, but by bringing the principles of Aristotelian and Platonic logic and philosophy into harmony with the many other principles he draws from the Old and New Testaments and from the teachings of the Fathers of the Church.

The doctrinal edifice of St Thomas can be conceived in a *pluralistic* way, as its multiple component principles dictate, whereas systems are always unitary or *monistic*. When Thales (625–545 BC) brings everything that exists back to water, when Anaximenes (585–525 BC) does the same with air, and Heraclitus (540–480 BC) with fire, they are striving for a *system*: their aim is to bring back to a *single* principle the multiplicity of appearances. For their part, Fichte, Hegel, and Schopenhauer do likewise, in that the first declares the "I," the second "Reason," and the third the "Will" to be the single all-embracing ruling principle. The difference between the two groups lies only in the fact that the three ancient Ionian philosophers drew their principles from outer experience, while the three Germans drew theirs from inner, psychological, experience. Common to them all, however, is the attempt to *bring back* to one thing the multiplicity of things (whether outer or inner)—which, as we have said, is the essence of system-building. By contrast, an order, or an edifice of doctrine (which is not in the least a system), is *directed towards* one thing, but *makes use of* a

111

multiplicity of principles in its quest to come closer to that one thing.

Now, every course of thinking, every striving for knowledge, is intent on an ultimate unity concealed behind the multiplicity of appearances, the unity revealed by means of those appearances. Indeed, the ultimate unity of the world is a postulate of "knowability" itself, for if in its essence the world were not a unity, knowledge as such would not even be possible. This is why the concern of every striving for knowledge is directed at discovering and knowing the unity lying concealed behind multiplicity, the unity made known by means of multiplicity. The *difference* in this respect between a system and an order is that a system elevates a single *experiential content* (or something deriving from that content) into the "principle" by means of which the multiplicity of experience is to be *explained*, whereas an order has to do with an *ultimate mystery* that it aims to *solve* by means of the multiplicity of experience.

A system knows *one* thing, and aims to explain *many* other things with its help; an order aims to solve *one* ultimate mystery, and to do so invokes *many* other things. Thus, the whole doctrinal edifice of St Thomas Aquinas has knowledge of the *mystery* of the Holy Trinity of God as its ultimate goal; it is ordered in such a way that, by making use of many things and methods (Scripture, the Fathers and Doctors of the Church, logic, and philosophy), he brings his readers ever closer to this goal. He establishes *many* secondary and partial insights stemming from the *one* mystery he is seeking to solve. Builders of systems proceed in quite another way: they take *one* thing as known or given, and, by reducing multiplicity (that is, many other things) to this one thing, propose to explain it with its help.

112

Whether this "one thing" underpinning and explaining multiplicity is discovered among such outer experiences as water, air, fire, or "matter," or among such inner, psychological experiences as "libido," "will to power," or "reason," makes no real difference: in each case, universal significance is ascribed to a single experiential content that gains prominence as an autocratic principle and comes to form the basis of a system.

⊕

"Systematic" thinking may in principle be described as a *mechanism*, whereas "ordered" thinking (if adequate to its content and thus, as it were, "fully grown") should instead be compared with an *organism*. Organic order *stems* from a series of independent investigations, and is as different as can be from systematic postulates, which, having been fixed from the beginning, determine the content of individual concepts. Organic order is a pattern of thoughts that emerges at the *end* of the process. In principle, moreover, such a pattern of thoughts can never be brought to an end: it remains open to further growth.

In systematic thinking, the content and value of each individual concept is determined by its *preconceived* ruling principle. By contrast, the *summarizing* proposition stemming (rather like a blossom or fruit) from ordered thinking is determined by the content of the individual concepts it takes under advisement in the course of its unfolding. Thus, for instance, the pattern of thought Kant set out for the world is *not* a system. It is, rather, a summation of his investigation of the theoretical capacity for knowledge, of practical moral consciousness, and of the power of aesthetic judgement—arrived at in three different ways, and yielding different and mutually conflicting results.

Kant is often reproached for having shown metaphysics out through one door (the *Critique of Pure Reason*) even as he ushered it back in through another (the *Critique of Practical Reason*)—and it is quite true that he did that. For in his view it was not a matter of some preconceived principle that "there must not be a metaphysics," but of an honest investigation of when and where metaphysics might be justified, and when and where it might not. In Kant's work there is no question of constructing a closed system, free from gaps and contradictions, in which metaphysics is to be ruled out on principle, but of a freely investigative labor of thought regarding just what can actually be achieved by the powers of human consciousness concerned with knowledge.

The fact that Kant came to the conflicting results that, on one hand, "human beings cannot say anything definite about God, freedom, and immortality," and on the other, that "human beings can say something definite about God, freedom, and immortality," is indeed a contradiction for those who construct systems; but it is absolutely not a contradiction for those seeking personal certainty. For the latter, the result of Kant's investigation of the *theoretical faculty* (i.e., that God, freedom, and immortality *cannot* in a purely theoretical way be either affirmed or denied) and the result that with the *moral faculty* God, freedom, and immortality *can* be asserted in a purely moral way, is just as natural and just as little a contradiction as the downward growth of a plant's root and the upward growth of its stalk would be unnatural, or a contradiction. These opposing directions of growth do not tear the plant in two! It is simply a question of the simultaneous working, in opposing directions, of two tendencies of the plant-organism. The root has no immediate experience of the effect of the sun, but does have the experience of the chemical and other properties of the soil. It is the stalk and its leaves that experience sunlight and air. This is a case of the plant-organism's different organs apportioning tasks and working together. The same is true for our cognitive organs: theoretical reason can say as little about God, freedom, and immortality as the plant's root can say about light and air; but practical reason *can* speak about God, freedom, and immortality, just as the plant-organism's stalk and leaves, could they talk, would have much to report about light and air.

Systematizers choose a single principle, a single method, and a single human capacity from which to fabricate their system. By contrast, seekers for personal certainty are oriented towards organic knowledge and make a point of calling upon as many methods and as many capacities for experience and knowledge as they have objects of knowledge or problems before them. In principle, each particular object of knowledge or each particular problem signifies for them the need to seek and to find a particular way or a particular method corresponding to this particular object or problem.

In the case of Kant's various doctrines, then, it is not a matter of taking the results of his work as limiting, but of appreciating the fact that he found it necessary to invoke different methods and different capacities of consciousness in order to aptly investigate different objects of knowledge. God, freedom, and immortality do not represent a merely theoretical concern, but a practical and a moral one as well, which appertains to the realm of moral, not formal, logic. This result on the part of Kant can be of significance for all thinking people. The same cannot be said, however, of the results of Kant's *application* of moral logic in his work. For if the moral logic of practical reason requires the existence of God, freedom, and immortality, why should it stop there rather than going on to further and deeper insights? Simply because it seemed to be enough for Kant's personal need for certainty, so that he took no further interest in exploring further? Surely not, for if we can attain to personal certainty about the existence of God, freedom, and immortality along the path of moral logic, it follows that this path may lead also to personal certainty about many other things in the supersensible realm. The path, thus opened, need only be *taken*.

⊕

A further distinction between system and order consists in the tendency of a system's concepts towards *monovalence* and *closure*, and the striving of an order's individual concepts toward *richness* in content and *openness*. For if, in a system, individual concepts are permitted only such content (and only as much of that content) as the ruling central principle of the system allows, the opposite is true of an order of thought that has grown organically: in the latter case, each concept has both a currently surveyable content and a "possible" content extending beyond it—a content that "for now" remains latent in the layers of the "sleeping consciousness," but may some day shine forth in waking consciousness also. Just as an iceberg consists of a part rising above the surface of the sea and a much larger part hidden in its depths, so too those concepts with which our consciousness works, not for the sake of a system but for their own sake, comprise a content that is both present above the surface in our waking consciousness and at the same lies hidden beneath its surface. Here, each concept has both a clear meaning and at the same time the possibility of manifold deeper meanings. Each such concept is in principle polyvalent in the sense of having the capacity to *intensify* its content in the direction of depth and heightened clarity.

For example, if our purpose is to take the concept of freedom, not as a link or a cog in a system, but in its own right, we will at first proceed purely phenomenologically. We will turn our attention to the manifold appearances and experiences of freedom, such as freedom of movement, freedom of action, freedom of choice, freedom of inquiry, freedom of thought, freedom of conscience; freedom from need, fear, and doubt, creative freedom, and still other kinds of freedom besides. Then we will seek a means of expressing what knowledge we may acquire in this way. We will not search for this means of expression, however, by ruling out other concepts, by establishing what freedom is *not* (and thereby arriving at a *definition*) but by communicating what freedom *is*, by *expressing* it. We will guard against considering the knowledge we have acquired in this way to be conclusive and finally valid. Rather, we will search out a means of expression that not only does justice to the insight we have thus far gained but that remains open-ended, affording room for further possible insights.

Now, a means of expression that meets these conditions can only be something emblematic: a *symbol*. For only symbols have the quality of expressing without defining, of communicating material content without formally delimiting, of remaining at once open in terms of content and susceptible to further deepening of interpretation.

The most essential difference between a sharply-defined concept and a symbol is that concepts strictly limited to a single meaning operate as links or cogs in a system's mechanism (behind which, as was pointed out before, lies a striving for power) and exercise a degree of *compulsion*, whereas symbols do not. Indeed, viewed from the perspective of what best suits the requirements of a system, the more *compellingly* restricted its constituent concepts are, the more perfect they are.

Thus, Fichte said that he wanted to *compel* his readers to acknowledge the truth of his teaching.[3] What he expressed in this way lives and works as the intention behind every "crystal-clear" conceptual line of argument. Therein lies as well one of the reasons the concept of "God" is held to be unscientific, as not bindingly and universally valid—that is, as not compelling assent in the way concepts held to be scientific are said to do. For this reason, all attempts to make God and God's existence compelling by means of such conceptual argument have fallen short. St Thomas Aquinas's *quinque viae* show that a person who believes in God *can* bring his reason into *accord* with this belief in five different ways, but they also show that they are not binding if taken as *proofs* for non-believers. The same holds true for Anselm's and Leibniz's more elaborate ontological proofs of God. Kant showed that these proofs lacked compelling bindingness. But even apart from Kant's critique of the proofs of God's existence, it is not hard to see that the acknowledgement or the denial of the existence of God is not, nor can it

[3] The text has "Hegel" here, but it was Hegel's contemporary J.G. Fichte who wrote the boldly-titled work the author appears to have in mind: "A Pellucid Report to the General Public concerning the Actual Essence of the Newest Philosophy: An Attempt to Compel the Reader to Understand," 1801.

be, a mere question of logical argumentation. Otherwise, there would never have been atheists who could think logically. Likewise, everyone who could not think with logical precision, or who did not trouble themselves with logical arguments, would be an atheist.

Kant himself put forward a credible reason for acknowledging God, but it is not a "proof" in the sense of exercising a compelling effect upon reason; it is, rather, a postulate of Kant's *moral* consciousness. Here it is not a question of the concept of "God" compelling us to acknowledge it; it is, instead, our own moral nature that requires this concept. Our moral nature imposes this concept, as it were, upon the world of concepts.

We might say that, insofar as the concept of God is not binding, it is already essentially *symbolic*. For symbols are emblems expressed by means of words, images, figures, and so on. They are, without question, significant, but binding they are not. The proposition "All men are mortal; Socrates is a man; therefore Socrates is mortal" *is* binding, whereas the proposition "On the third day he rose again; he ascended into heaven; he is seated at the right hand of the Father, and he will come to judge the living and the dead" *is not* binding, but is, rather, a declaration. In other terms, the first proposition says "You are not free to acknowledge or not to acknowledge my logic; you have unequivocally and without reservation to acknowledge what I mean." The second proposition says, "Look, here I set before you things of great value and of deep significance. Come, if you will, come closer, come into their light, warmth, and life." The first proposition commands. The second proposition offers, like an invitation to dine. It does not order or command; it only recommends and offers. This is precisely the universal spirit of symbolism: offering without commanding.[4]

Symbolism leaves us free; it is the language in which free person speaks to free person. In symbolism, respect for freedom goes further than the freedom merely to accept or to reject what is offered in the symbol: even *after* accepting (or, more precisely, receiving) a symbol, we are still free. For the symbol does not impose a particular content or a monovalent concept; instead, it offers a path and a means to *discoveries* that we can only make for ourselves *within* it. It is polyvalent. Its multiplicity of meanings is not indeterminacy, however, but consists, rather, in the inner *layering* of the content specified by the symbol.

The symbol is a path to deepening; it yields content upon content, stored in layers within it. These contents are only acquired through free initiative and personal discovery on the part of the consciousness intent on deepening itself. Any symbol *can* remain monovalent for a particular person, if that person is satisfied with a single layer of meaning and seeks no further deepening. But even then, the monovalent concept or content gained from the symbol is that person's *own* discovery. A symbol can be understood in a superficial or in a profound way, but in either case we remain free, not only in the sense that we are free to understand it either superficially or profoundly, but also in the sense that the content gained is our *own* discovery, even if myriad other people have found the same content in it.

---

[4] "To offer": *bieten*. "To command": *ge-bieten*.

⊕

Can symbols be *interpreted*? They certainly can, and they ought to be, for therein consists their life and their significance as a means of expression. But we should be on our guard against thinking of one particular interpretation as *the* interpretation, and declaring it to be such! The present author has been concerned with symbolism his whole life long, but to this day has never had the feeling that he has given the final interpretation of even a single symbol, i.e., that he has exhausted the content of any symbol. Moreover, he has arrived at the conviction that although interpreting symbols in the language of clearly contoured concepts can be justified and even welcomed, such interpretations can never replace the symbols themselves—can never "interpret them away."

Thus, we can certainly interpret the symbol of the cross as "sacrifice," but this interpretation of the symbol does not exhaust its meaningfulness. The cross also symbolizes the vertical and horizontal tendencies in the growth of plants, which results in the spiral line characterizing illustrations of the branches and leaves of plants. Then again, it symbolizes the law of the growth of human consciousness along the dimensions of height and breadth, from which results a spiral form of development (for yes, our path as human beings is specified by the cross). Furthermore, the cross is an emblem of our two primary duties, which stand in eternal contradiction with one another: to remain at our post in life and to set out into the distance as pilgrims. Indeed, our duty as human beings *is* a cross. The cross is likewise a monitory sign of our task of bearing, enduring, and resolving the contradiction between ideal and reality; for, on its own, the vertical is Don Quixote, and the horizontal is Sancho

Panza. The full *human being*, however, is a cross. The cross signifies at the same time the primary tasks of thinking, of philosophy, and of comprehending the opposition between idealism and realism in an "ideal-realism"—for human thinking *is* a cross. Then again, the cross signifies both the spiritual and the bodily principle of health in human beings, the capacity for passivity and for activity, for sleeping and for waking. Yes, human life is a cross. The cross likewise signifies the simultaneous necessity of devotion to the world and humanity, and of solitude and independence in our understanding and in matters of conscience.[5] Our social dealings form a cross. The cross signifies space and time, causality and freedom, heredity and individuality, matter and spirit, life and death, and much else besides. All in all, human destiny in the world is a cross.

Symbolism is not only the language of being free and of leaving free; it is the language of creative productivity and of true modesty. For we only have an opportunity and a reason to make use of symbolism if, for the sake of knowledge and expression, we wish to create out of the depths—i.e., if our waking consciousness and the deeper layers of our consciousness (our "sleeping consciousness") stimulate each other. At the same time, we will always be reminded by the nature and meaning of symbolism itself that we are pupils, and will remain so always. The most we can offer to others, to our fellow pupils in the great school of life, is an individually stimulating example of how to learn, and how learning enriches life.

[5] "Understanding": *Wissen*. "Conscience": *Ge-wissen*.

Symbolism preserves us from presumption. Thus the Holy Trinity, although the symbol of the highest mystery of divinity, in the sense of the inexhaustibility of its knowledge and of the light contained in it (not in the sense of darkness), produces modesty. Our thinking, too, can adopt a kneeling posture; and we genuflect in just this way every time we ponder the Holy Trinity. By contrast, the effect of credulity towards a system intent on power is quite different. The doctrine of the dialectical "trinity" of thesis, antithesis, and synthesis can give rise to the presumptuous delusion of knowing everything; or, put another way, of knowing better about everything. Hegel spoke in the name of the world-spirit; Marx spoke in the name of world-history; Lenin and Stalin believed that, as masters of dialectic, they had total knowledge. In short, whereas the more fully we honor the Holy Trinity, the more significance it acquires for our consciousness, the more fully we acquire mastery in handling the dialectical triad, the more admiration we claim for ourselves.

Now, it needs saying that it is certainly not impossible to transform symbols into monovalent concepts (i.e., to "de-symbolify" them) and then piece them together into a system. This is in fact just what gives rise to rigid theological systems, systems that often enough not only lead to inhuman cruelty but to monstrous slanders against God. It was just this process of "de-symbolifying" symbols into impoverished concepts that gave rise to the particular theological system that sees God as having predestined one segment of humanity to eternal blessedness and another to eternal damnation. This nonsensical proposition, which stands out in its prodigious immorality when torn from its context in the theological system we are speaking of, nevertheless follows with iron-clad inexorability within that system, raised up as it is upon the ruling principle of God's omnipotence and omniscience... from which, however, with never a word, love has been excluded.

⊕

Now, just as it is possible to "de-symbolify" symbols and make monovalent concepts of them, so is it possible to deepen monovalent concepts and transform them into symbols—to "symbolify" them. This is how arithmetical concepts of number and numerical relationships, and geometrical concepts of space and spatial relationships, were transformed into symbols. Such symbols played an important part in the thought of the Pythagoreans, the Gnostics, and the Kabbalists, as well as in Plato's dialogue *Timaeus*, where the One was understood as unity, which stood in turn for the origin of all becoming, as well as the final goal and ideal of all knowing. Arithmetic in no way suffered from this "symbolification," for its rules continued to apply unaltered, irrespective of whether they did or did not have a superadded symbolic meaning. The transformation we are speaking of did not concern the structure or the laws of arithmetic or of geometry, but only their *significance* for human beings: to their quantitative significance was added a qualitative one.

By virtue of this "symbolification" of monovalent concepts, mathematics also acquired, alongside its function of calculating quantities, that of being a stimulus to knowledge of the essential constituents of being. Is it nonsense and foolery to think of one as unity, two as separation or polarization, and three as overcoming separation? Or again, take the algebraic expression: $a + b = c$. It is purely formal;

its letters stand for arbitrary *quantities*. By contrast, let us take a sentence from the Kabbalah: "Beauty originates in the unification of severity and mildness." In the language of the Kabbalah the sentence reads "*Tiferet* originates in the unification of *Geburah* and *Gedulah*." The second proposition is purely substantive; its words stand for particular *qualities*. Yet both propositions actually say the same thing: the unification of two factors or values yields a third.

The essential difference between the two propositions essentially consists in the fact that the first is without qualities, i.e., is morally *dead*, while the second, even though it does also include quantitative aspect, is focused entirely on the qualitative, i.e., on *life*. Symbolism is the purely qualitative language of knowledge, and is therefore the language of *life*. The quantitative language of mathematics and mechanics is the language of *death*. In this sense, the gospel teaching that "heaven and earth shall pass away, but my words shall not pass away" can also be read as "however extensive heaven or the earth may be, as quantities they belong to the realm of death; but my words are not quantities and do not belong to the realm of passing-away, for they are life, they are quality."

Much more of essential importance could be said about symbolism and its significance for the path to personal certainty. And this we shall undertake to do so in the further course of this general exposition of the practical problem of knowledge without compulsion, which has thus far led us to consider the nature of system, order, and symbol. For the present, however, let us introduce two concrete examples that will lend "flesh and blood" to what has so far been suggested and should also prove to be of value in our further contemplation of this problem. The following examples relate to the use of a moral, qualitative thinking corresponding to "moral logic," and also—by means of formal, aesthetic, and moral thinking—to the use of symbolism as a means on the path towards deepening the content of this moral logic.

First Digression: *"A Credo."* An Example of the Moral and Qualitative Way of Considering Things

Organized, living, and conscious beings with particular forms surround me in the world. Where did they come from? What lies behind them? When I meet adult human beings, I know that they owe their lives as adults to the fact that, after they were born, loving hands received and cared for them until they reached an age at which they acquired the ability to look after themselves. People are not born equipped to sustain their life: a nursling left alone must soon die. Thus, all human beings owe their lives to love.

Is this the case only with human beings? Can anything be created, built, or acquired out of indifference, even out of hatred? Can a piece of music be composed out of indifference or hatred towards music? Can a world of organized, living, and conscious beings with a particular form originate out of indifference or hatred towards that world? After all, indifference is by nature uncreative, and hatred destructive. Where else than in love can the force that gives the beings of the world their existence, and that is revealed in the creatively formative activity of the world, be found?

If there is a creative, a formative, element at work in the world (and there is, since becoming and taking shape are at play therein), how is it possible that absolute indifference (the *materia* of the materialists) could work itself up to such achievements? Were it to do so, it would no longer *be* indifference! It would be love, for only love wishes to give and to form being.

Or are we to believe that the creative, formative element in the world is a blind, dark, drive, that does not wish to *give* being but rather to *get* being for itself—that wants to give form to and beget itself? But is not even a blind, dark drive that brings into being the finely organized eyes and that creates brains (the brains that it, the "unthinking," uses to think with) a drive to form, to organize, to create—i.e., is it not a drive that *loves* this existence, *loves* this being, and *loves* this formative activity? Even if we are only willing to grant this drive a bare minimum of content (the minimum granted it by evolutionists), it is still nothing other than love, even if a blind and bare love. The drive for life or development of which people speak either has no content at all, or else its content is some degree of love, however small. Were this not so, the drive we are speaking of would have been unable to create anything; indeed, it would not have *wanted* to create anything—as a *drive*, it would not have existed at all!

The world came into being out of love. It lives through love and is preserved by love. If we call what creates and preserves in the world "God," then God is love, and whoever lives in love, lives in God, and God in him.

Love is not a substance like air or water, something that exists, flows, or wends its way only for itself. It is a relationship, an attitude. Love always presupposes a lover. And since love cannot be compelled, the lover is free from the world. But a being who is free, we call a *person*. Thus God is a person, and as a creation of love, the world is God's free act. God is freedom, and whoever lives in God lives in freedom and is free. Since God is a free person, the being of human beings and of other conscious beings is a free act of God. It is a *gift*. Since this gift is of God, it is not lent us for a time, to be demanded back later, but is given for all eternity. The being of the human person is, then, everlasting. The human person is immortal. As God is a person and is immortal, so whoever is a person is immortal like God.

God does not give what He *possesses*, but what He *is*. He gives being, true being. But true being is personhood alone. And so, our personhood is the image of God's personhood. It is not the case that God, as a person, is an anthropomorphizing projection on our part. Rather, we, as persons, are a theomorphizing projection of God. As God is the most personal person, all the qualities of our human personhood have their pattern in God. If our love in God corresponds to a divine love, then also: our joy too corresponds to a divine joy; our suffering to a divine suffering; our anger to a divine anger; our hope to a divine hope; our laughter to a divine smile; our tears to divine tears…

God is the fullness of life. And the fullness of life is full personhood. Whoever lives a full life of human personhood lives a life in the likeness of the life of God. For we are the image and likeness of God. This implies as well that we are endowed with the gift of creativity. Imitation is the first stage of creation; alteration or re-shaping[6] is the second; giving form to unformed raw matter is the third. The last and highest stage is creation out of *nothing*. Our creative imagination can certainly create out of the fullness of what

---

[6] *Umgestaltung.*

exists, out of existence; but it can also create out of nothingness, out of the void of non-existence. If we engage our
creative imagination in and through the fullness of existence, it gives birth to the unborn; if, however, we direct our
creative imagination to the void of non-existence, it con-
jures a novel existence[7] alien to divinely-bestowed existence—to which it stands in opposition as a counter-
existence. This is how evil comes into the world; and with
it: isolation, sickness, and death. Out of nothingness, personalities (human or other) create counter-worlds within
the world of God. This is how conflict comes to pass in the
world between the divinely-willed creation and a "counter-
creation" altered and reshaped, or recreated, by the arbitrary will of such personalities.

Natural scientists, who have come to know much of the life
of nature, tell us that nature is neither good nor evil. With
one hand, she bestows life and happiness; and with the
other, she cruelly destroys them. Nature, they say, is amoral
and without intention: she pursues her game of life and
death not only with tender creativeness rich in love, but
with cruel destructiveness also. With sublime indifference
she fits the wondrous cooperation of bees and flowers to the
purposes of life, or the wisely precautionary organization of
the mammary glands to the nourishment of mammalian
infants and young. With this same indifference she also creates the tetanus bacillus in the soil, the agents of poliomyeli-
tis in the ground and water, and in stagnant pools the
malaria bacillus, which invades the blood by means of mos-

[7] *Sein.*

quitoes and midges, killing well over a million people every year in India alone. What natural scientists call "nature" is at once kind and cruel… But does this "nature" they speak of actually exist? Is not what they call by that name only an abstraction drawn from a *series* of regulating principles and "worlds" pitched into the one pot of this abstraction?

What in this way is most often called *nature* is in fact the external *scene* on which "kindly-wise" nature meets "distorted" nature, and "fantastically arbitrary" nature. Bees and flowers belong to a *different* realm of being than do malaria microbes; tigers and hyenas to still another. If we are to parse the manifold of "nature," at least three realms of existence must therefore be distinguished: kindly-wise nature; distorted nature; and destructive, evil nature.

These three realms are engaged in an ongoing battle with each other that could in no way be called nature *per se*— i.e., nature unified. We cannot say of a battle that it is "neutral" or "purposeless" solely because soldiers on both sides perish. Likewise, we cannot say that nature is "amoral" and "malicious" solely because she "destroys with one hand what she has created with the other." Just as a battle is not a unified organism, but a conflict between armies that come to the field of battle from different directions, so "nature" is not a unified organism, but is the scene both of cooperation *and* of conflict between realms of being of quite different provenance. Or will someone claim that God devised malarial microbes, deployed them in stagnant pools, and commissioned them to enlist midges to help end millions of human lives in torment? May God be blamed for the creation of parasites? Is there not a much greater moral logic in what Goethe has Mephistopheles say?

Lord of rats and lord of mice,
Of flies and frogs and bugs and lice,
Does he bid you—rat—to dare
Gnaw with your teeth this threshold here?

Here we find clearly expressed the thought that alongside
the Divine Creation other creations join the field. Were this
not so, we should have to deny the contribution of humanity to nature in the world's great cities, and say "God created New York, London, and Moscow." Now, we know
well enough that these cities are the work of human beings;
but how many things might there be in the world whose
origin we do not know, and for which on this account we
most often ascribe responsibility to God or to His nature?
After all, God gave to many beings the capacity to create,
which they use in different ways. That is why, within the
overarching framework of all Creation, contradictions and
oppositions exist.

What goes for so-called nature goes also for world history, which is ruled not only by *God*, but also by the freedom and the arbitrary will of the beings who participate in
forming and determining it, with fateful consequences.
Providence, freedom, and fate, as consequences of the use
or misuse of freedom in the past, are revealed simultaneously on the field of world history. World history thus
embraces both progress and regress, regeneration and
degeneration. It is a *cross*. Not only humanity's cross, but
God's as well. For by granting freedom to beings, God
restricted His own freedom. Insofar as it is ruled by free
beings, world history has become God's cross. God is crucified in world history.

Anyone who *cannot* see this, or who does not want to see
this, will sooner or later either deny God or blaspheme

against Him by holding Him responsible for all the coerced subjugation and injustice of world history. Anyone who *can* see this, and who is willing to see it, will sooner or later say: "We human beings have made world history like this; You, however, wanted it to be otherwise. Think of me, when Your kingdom comes." Amid the vicissitudes of world history, three crosses stand fast: the cross of human fate, the cross of human arbitrary will, and the cross of God's providence. Two thieves, and a "third" between them: this is the moral image that stands behind the outer events of world history. God's grave is being dug ever and again somewhere in the world. And somewhere in the world a form of God's resurrection is occurring ever and again. And ever and again a sort of ascension, ever and again a sort of pentecost also...

World history seen from a purely *moral* point of view is the history of God in human consciousness: born, crucified, buried, resurrected, ascended towards heaven, and descended like a beacon into the human interior. These are the essential events with which world history is concerned; without them, it would be an unending nightmare without aim or meaning. The Church sets this aim or meaning of world history before humanity every day and every year. The Church is the visible backbone of world history. It is the organ of the consciousness of the unity of humanity's vocation. Humanity is called, with God, to life's triumph over death. These things stand before moral consciousness in a manner such that it cannot be otherwise. For personal moral consciousness they are certain: "certainly true."

Second Digression: *Measure, Number, and Weight.*
An Example of the Application of Symbolism

All things can be grasped *qualitatively*. When they are, they become symbols. This is also true of such concepts as "measure, number, and weight," which are usually understood only in a quantitative sense—indeed, they are considered the original, defining concepts *of* quantity. In being grasped qualitatively, they do not, however, relinquish their quantitative meaning—for although quantity does not include quality, quality *does* include quantity. That is, symbolism includes not only what is measurable, countable, and weighable, but also what is valuable, precious, and impressive.

Quantity is the *corpse* of quality. To determine the number of people in a nation, the individuals to be counted must be thought of as lifeless, rather as one counts corpses. If I say that a nation numbers forty million people, nothing more is said regarding these people than if it were a question of forty million corpses. When the people are counted, the individual, living elements are stripped away from them, and what remains are corpses, i.e., people who have become things. What has been said regarding number holds true as well for measure and weight when they are used in an exclusively quantitative sense. Lifeless things such as corpses can not only be counted, they can be weighed and measured also. But as has been said, measure, number, and weight can also be understood in a qualitative way, that is, *symbolically*, for attributes and values are susceptible of "intensification" also. They too can have their "more" and their "less." Thoughts and deeds likewise have their "weight." There are weighty decisions, and opinions that carry weight, that we cannot accept "lightly." Before

133

coming to a weighty decision, we also "weigh in" for and against. Or again, we speak of the "measure" of our interest in certain things, and of the measure of our patience. We carry the "burden" of responsibility and suffer under the "onus" of an awareness of guilt.

Weight and Faith. When we say that we "lay weight upon something," we mean that we take it seriously, that we are ready to bestow more attention upon the relevant thing, matter, or question than upon other things, matters, and questions on which we lay no particular weight. To lay weight on something means to take something seriously; and to take something seriously has the practical significance that we apply a greater quantity of *concentration* to it. Now, the ability to concentrate our attention, or to "hoard—to await the ripening hour—in the least point the loftiest power" (Goethe)[8] is the ability to take things seriously as such.

Those who in their thoughts, feelings, and wishes pass things by without pause *cannot* take things seriously because those things become like insubstantial ghosts hurrying past them, even though it is actually *they* who in their thoughts hurry past *them*. Things then lose their property of *leaving an impression* upon consciousness. Thoughts, ideas, and ideals likewise lose their property of making an impression on any consciousness unable or unwilling to bring to bear upon them the necessary degree of attention, of concentration. What are the collections of art treasures in the Prado, the Louvre, the British Museum, or the Zwinger (in Dresden) worth to those who pay no attention to them

---

[8] These lines are not actually from Goethe, but from Schiller's poem *Breadth and Depth.*

because their attention is concentrated wholly upon themselves? What is the value of John's gospel to those who have never read it with their full attention—that is, to those who have never read or heard it properly at all?

"Blessed are the poor in spirit, for theirs is the kingdom of heaven"—because they are unpreoccupied and therefore able to give their undivided attention to new things of value, and to treasure them. For those whose consciousness, whose "spirit," is not "poor" (not free and open) but "rich" (full of what belongs to them, uninterested in and unappreciative of what is different and new), the kingdom of the highest values, the kingdom of heaven, is insubstantial and without value. They have nothing left for the kingdom of heaven because they are completely taken up with their own "kingdom," with which their attention, their capacity to concentrate, is completely bound up. They have "no ear with which to hear," because, even were they to hear the proclamation of the highest truths and of the greatest values with their physical ear, they would not notice anything. Their attention being directed elsewhere, the proclamation would not make any impression on them, and the highest truths and the greatest values thus proclaimed would carry no weight for them. They would not have taken them seriously.

The capacity to bring our total attention to bear on thoughts, ideas, and ideals, to take them really seriously, is, in the end, the *capacity for faith*. For the act of taking hold of faith consists in taking a thought seriously and experiencing the *weight* (i.e., the great value) of its content and the impression it makes. The capacity for faith rests upon the ability to be impressed by ideas, to experience their *weight*.

Those who do not bring their whole attention and openness to bear on thoughts, ideas, and ideals will never experience their *weight*. They may indeed bring relativistically held opinions, suppositions, and hypotheses to bear on them, but they will be unable to take hold of faith. Faith is not an opinion upon which one insists, but is instead like the imprinting of a seal on the whole of a person's consciousness, which is made good by its *weight*. The so-called "Numenosum"[9] of Rudolf Otto and C.G. Jung (which designates sealing in faith in the religious domain, and conversion in the psychological field) is another word for the effect of the *weight* of thoughts, ideas, and ideals on human consciousness. The *experience* of faith is the experience of the weight of spiritual things.

Measure and Hope. A similar deepening in the direction of the qualitative can take place with the concept of "measure." Here too we can start from daily experience. We all know that we have a certain measure of patience, that we can only bear something painful, oppressive, or boring to such and such an extent or for this or that length of time. But we can also have the experience that the measure of what we can bear grows considerably if it is a question of bearing it for the sake of a higher value, if it has a "meaning." If we have in mind something in the future, something by which we set great store—and if we possess the ability to keep this future something continually before our eyes—the measure of what is bearable to us grows enor-

[9] See C.G. Jung, *Psychology and Religion* (New Haven, CT, 1937) and Rudolf Otto, *The Idea of the Holy: An Inquiry into the Non-rational Factor in the Idea of the Divine and Its Relation to the Rational* (Oxford: OUP, 1952). VT

mously. We put up with much more from a child than we do from an adult, because we know a child carries a future being within, for whose sake it is worth putting up with present poor behavior. It is *hope* that enables the measure of our endurance to grow. All the martyrs and silent sufferers created their power to endure from this source, the source of hope.

The capacity for hope determines the measure of what we can bear. It presupposes that we are able to make something in the future present to ourselves so vividly that, in effect, it becomes part of the present. It is the capacity to "remember the future." Just as gratitude presupposes the capacity to see something valuable in the past, despite everything that distracts us from it (or even everything that contradicts it), and *not to forget* this valuable thing, so hope is the capacity *not to forget* a possible thing of value in the future. It is, so to say, gratitude in advance. And our capacity for gratitude in advance, our capacity to make a future thing of value present to ourselves, is our *measure*—the span of time we can wait, endure, and hold out. Hope is the measure of the *strength* of the life of our soul, of the capacity of our consciousness not to lose heart, not to give up, not to capitulate.

Number and Love. If we now deepen in the same manner the concept of number or "counting" in the direction of the qualitative, we come first upon the fact that there are people who "count" for us, and others who "count" less, or not at all. We become aware that, as regards our *psychic reality*, in the end only a certain number of people really exist (i.e., "count") to the degree that we have in some form or manner received them into our hearts. Only a person we love can count in this way. Thus our qualitative "count" measures the extent of our capacity to love. The count of the complete egoist is *one*, since for him he himself is all that really exists.

Whenever a Thou becomes a psychic reality for me, whether in friendship or in love, I make the great and often shattering step from one to two. Now I am no longer alone; my psychic reality has extended itself to the Thou. And every further "count" means a further coming out of myself, a further expansion of my psychic reality.

The ancient Pythagoreans said that numbers were gods. If by "gods" is meant "extending *beyond* human beings," number is in fact something that lifts and extends us above and beyond our own limitedness. "Numbers are gods," because gods are *more* than us and because numbers stand for the "more" that is present whenever we human beings go beyond ourselves. In loving, we live a life that is *more* than our own life. The *capacity for love* is the life of number, and the life in number is divine. The number of beings in the world is an expression of God's love. The number of beings in the world is great, because God's love is great.

⊕

Thus can a deepened (i.e., a qualitative or symbolic) examination of weight, measure, and number, lead to their interiorization as faith, hope, and love.

V

Theology and Personal Certainty

HE FOREGOING DISCUSSION OF COGNITIVE LIFE in general and the path to personal certainty has been concerned with scientific and philosophical matters in particular. Now it is time to consider *theological matters* too, as they relate to the striving for personal certainty. From the side of the traditional Church, seekers after personal certainty are told that faith in the authority of the Church is necessary. They can at first understand "the authority of the Church" in only two ways. Firstly, there were once spiritual and bodily events that became the content of a tradition. Secondly, this tradition survives unadulterated within the Church to this day. Considering the Church's claim to authority in this light, we cannot avoid admitting that the claim to the *authority of testimony* is indeed well-founded. For we cannot deny the presence of the tradition and have to recognize that the content of this tradition possesses a very great power of conviction, since it has continued uninterrupted for so long.

Now, testimonial witness, especially conjoined with the degree of conviction the Church has garnered in the course of its history, serves, in principle, to establish trust. One may not *want* to trust such witness for personal reasons of some kind, but the strict law of objective justice (which is

139

operative in the court proceedings of all the countries of the free world) holds that one is obliged to believe a witness, so long as what that witness affirms has not been irrefutably demonstrated to be untrue. In any event, an approach that mistrusts the Church in advance, just like the same sort of approach towards science or philosophy, is completely unfruitful. For trust is openness, and openness is the precondition of learning. Getting to know and understand someone or something is impossible without respect and openness. Sceptics know nothing important about the world or about life, not because the world and life contain nothing important to know about, but because they are sceptics—i.e., because they are not open to what is important in them.

The sense of justice, then, requires that I should bestow no less trust upon the Church as a witness than I bestow upon astronomers who tell me about objects in outer space that I have not seen for myself. This trust, however, would be meaningless if it were *blind*. I can only trust things that I have gotten to know myself. But not much is achieved by merely knowing the Judeo-Christian tradition if I do not understand it, i.e., if I do not *myself* attain to an insight into its truth-content and value. A mere repetition of the words "I believe in God the Father almighty, Maker of heaven and earth," is not asked of me; what is asked of me is that I should say these words in such a way that they are the expression of *my personal conviction*. These words can only be an expression of my personal conviction, however, if I have personal certainty that their content is true. I may be infinitely grateful to the Church for having kept the tradition going and for having brought it to me, and I may repose the greatest trust in the Church, but this in no way relieves me of the task of actually and honestly bringing that which I have received with trust and gratitude to personal certainty as well. For anything I do not understand or experience or grasp in some other way *cannot* be believed by me, since it is impossible to believe merely in words, but only in thoughts, values, beings, and events. But then, we can only believe in thoughts, values, beings, and events if they are susceptible of being thought, felt, and willed—that is, if through insight, sympathy, and setting upon them a moral value, they have become (even if only to a modest degree) the objects of personal certainty.

If such were not the case, *theology* would never have come into being at all. For the concern of theology is precisely to make the content of the revelation handed down by tradition *intelligible* in a non-contradictory manner. The concern of theology is to bring the content of revelation closer to thinking in this way, just as it is brought closer to the heart and to the will by means of worship.

The theological *method* consists in bringing the intellect to bear on the revelation handed down by tradition, on the presupposition that this revelation is a reality, and that it itself, and not my understanding of it, is *true*. Natural science also applies itself to nature on the presupposition that natural appearances are real and express a *true* law-governed character. The articles of revelation are to the theologian what the facts of nature are to the natural scientist. Natural scientists direct their thinking towards natural objects and allow that thinking to be corrected and instructed by the facts. For the natural scientist, the facts of nature constitute not merely the object of research but also its criterion, its highest authority, and its final court of appeal. Likewise, for the theologian it is the statements of the revelation handed

141

down by tradition that constitutes the object, the criterion, and the highest authority for research. Nature is the "bible" of the natural scientist; the theologian's "nature" is the Bible. Both start out from the assumption that the "natural revelation" in nature and the "supernatural revelation" in the Bible are not vain lies and deception, but realities and truths. Work in both these directions on the basis of this positive assumption has shown itself to be fruitful. The results of the natural sciences are owed to an attitude of belief towards the revelation of nature; the results of the theological sciences (dogmatics, exegesis, apologetics, moral theology, ecclesiastical history, comparative religion, pastoral theology, liturgiology, canon law, and so on) are owed to an attitude of belief towards supernatural revelation.

The development of theology over the course of nineteen centuries shows that it has done an astonishing intellectual job. Even if, as in everything that lives and that is capable of life, there have been different (indeed opposed) tendencies continually at work in it (such as positive and negative theology, a legalistic-formal tendency, and a symbolic-mystical tendency), theology has nevertheless raised up a thought-edifice not only of imposing dimensions but also worked out with the most careful attention to individual details. Generations at once devout and intelligent have worked with enormous diligence and self-sacrifice on this thought-edifice, adding to it stone upon stone, chiseling each individual concept to its sharpest possible definition.

Ever since John Damascene (by way of Alexander of Hales, Albertus Magnus, Thomas Aquinas, Duns Scotus, and Bonaventure, through to our own day) a thought-temple has been erected in theology that stands before our inner sense with the same majesty as that with which the great cathedrals stand open to the outer senses. If we rightly prize the great buildings of the Gothic age, the great cathedrals that stand before our outer senses, and marvel at the artistic sensibility and the diligence of those who built them, why do we not bring the same reverence to the great thought-edifice, or feel the same wonder at the enthusiasm, sense of form, and diligence of *its* architects?

The reason is of course that, whereas it is not difficult for us moderns to view the cathedrals of our forebears in physical space and allow them to have their effect upon us, in order to see and appreciate the invisible cathedrals of *thought*, we must ourselves have actively pursued *in thought* all the features of their architecture. To do this, we must have carried out an intellectual task very few are in-clined to undertake. Nevertheless, justice bids us to honor the intellectual buildings of our ancestors as highly as we honor their visible buildings; that we pay our deserved respects not only to the great architects in stone and their hard-working masons, but equally to the intellectual builders. We will hardly be able to refuse such intellectual builders our respect if we remember that their real concern was to take seriously not only a revelation handed down by tradition, but human thinking also. The seriousness with which they took both religion and the value they set upon human thinking (along with their skilled handling of that thinking) can make a deep impression on modern people; it can, indeed, put them to shame.

The Scholastics (especially the earlier ones) display a seriousness such as is today almost only ever possessed by *children*: an intact hundred-percent-seriousness undisturbed by relativism. To get an idea of the spirit of Scholasticism, we need only picture to ourselves a child whose innocent eagerness has not yet been dissipated by education and experience, and then give this child the understanding of an adult. The ironically mocking sense of the worldling, the so-called worldly wisdom of a Montaigne, a François de la Rochefoucauld, a Voltaire, even a Bertrand Russell today (to whom everything appears relative and more or less discredited), is foreign to the spirit of Scholasticism. The child knows no mockery: he is convinced, and he wishes to convince others.

For all that, however, the Scholastics were in no way primitive, or but little touched by culture. To the contrary, their works testify to their prodigious sophistication, to an intellectual life and command of language attained through discipline and practice. Most of the concepts we have inherited from Scholasticism and use almost without thinking about them (such as "form" and "matter," "substance" and "essence") were originally deep and rich in content. They were true intellectual achievements of a depth, clarity, and refinement of thought. How often do we meet anyone today who clearly understands the distinction between the concepts "substance" and "essence," for example?

Those whose thinking is schooled to grasp such concepts and to possess such refinement in distinguishing between them, are not primitive! They are people of culture through and through. It is only that their ideal of culture was different from ours today. Theirs was the ideal of a *theocentric* culture, whereas the ideal of culture that rules today is *anthropocentric*. The highest representatives of medieval culture wished to base it on God and on His revelation, whereas the best representatives of modern culture base their culture on human beings alone.

⊕

Today, a powerful tendency is already at work trying to instate a third ideal of culture, that of the economic order. Socialism is oriented towards neither God nor the human being as person, but towards the social and political economic order. Just as today Kant means nothing to a member of the Academy of Sciences in the USSR, so Thomas Aquinas or Duns Scotus mean nothing to a neo-Kantian.

Seekers after personal certainty do not, however, ask whether they should accept this or that ideal of culture. Their concern is, rather, with attaining personal certainty in the eternal questions facing the human race. They cannot join a "movement of the day" (whether old or new) and allow themselves to be carried along by it. If they did this, they would have given up their *own* ideal of personal certainty, for if they were to swim along with some such movement, they would have turned their *personal* concerns into a *collective* one. They are not *indifferent* towards individual historical ideals of culture; their approach is to be *free* with respect to them, to "test them and conserve the best."

This holds equally true for the cultural ideals of antiquity, the middle ages, and the modern era. The reason for this is not that cultural ideals are transient, but precisely the opposite: because cultural ideals are *eternal*; because each of them possesses a *part* of eternity. They all live on (whether in the outer layer of consciousness, or in the deeper layers) and are always "present." Everything in them of eternal value, everything true in them, remains standing, remains always and everywhere "current."

Cultural ideals remain as layers of consciousness, even for those who have never read any books about them. And whenever a deeper-lying layer of consciousness makes its presence felt in the outer layer, a "renaissance" occurs—whether of the middle ages, of antiquity, or of other still more distant cultural epochs. Just as a tree trunk *consists* of the rings marking its life history, so also consciousness *consists* of the layers of its life-history—the only difference being that these layers do not harden into wood but are instead realized in their continuing effect upon each other. The ideals of chivalry, for example, live on in and among us even if we no longer carry sword or shield, or wear a helmet. So also do the ideals of the great buildings consecrated to God live in and among us—by which we mean not only the visible cathedrals of stone but also the intellectual cathedrals, the *summas* of Scholasticism. This is true for all things past that possess an eternal value. A chivalry or craft masonry that is truly consecrated to God carries the breath of eternal value within. There will be knights and master masons, then—and saints too—for as long as human beings on earth are able to develop in freedom.

Alongside this "eternal past," however, are also manifestations of the "ephemeral past" that possess no eternal value. The past lives on solely through that in it which is stronger than forgetting, sleep, and death: that which has eternal value. But the past also more often calls to mind the artificial life of an unhallowed and unredeemed *phantom*. On the one hand, the past *lives* as an eternal value; on the other, it *haunts* us as an unsatisfied passion, a demand, a pretension. The great empires of the past haunt us in the form of a power-craving complex for absolute domination that in our day takes possession not only of leaders but also of the masses whom they lead. This complex haunts us as well in the form of "absolute systems" such as Marxism-Leninism. In tandem with the state's machinery for coer-

146

cion, such systems are means to exercise power over the life of thought. The same power-craving complex haunts us in absolute *systems* and totalitarian political *regimes* alike. Even the middle ages (especially the later middle ages and the so-called early modern period) was not free from the specter of absolute power. This specter was fully engaged in the political conflict between the pope and the emperor; but it was no less active in the area of theology and law.

⊕

In theology, alongside the noble building of the intellectual temple in God's honor, an effort also made itself felt to elaborate a comprehensive, ironclad "system" with which to bring people's minds and hearts and ways of life under its control. This ploy to divert theology from its original, authentic concern (to bring revelation closer to conscious understanding) ended by providing a foothold to a transmogrified "theological system" that lay claim to exclusive power over all prescriptive and proscriptive *legal norms.* From then on, this system undertook to lay down a codified body of law governing thinking as such, stipulating exhaustively how each person ought and ought *not* to think about everything essential to the world and to the fate of humanity. To begin with, the coercive power of this "theological system" was to derive from its lack of contradiction or gaps; later, however, when the coercion of such internal coherence and systematicity proved insufficient, it was supplemented by outward means—those of the Inquisition.

Every system that lays claim to exclusive power is in principle filled with the spirit of the Inquisition and in practice (whenever circumstances allow) creates an "inquisitional machinery." The inquisitional machinery of the Marxist-

Leninist system is just as natural a product of such systemically exclusive power as was the Gestapo of the National Socialist system (a system that was admittedly nebulous, but nevertheless laid claim to exclusive power). Inquisitions are as old as claims to exclusive power on the part of systems of any kind. The Inquisition of the later middle ages went together with the legal and political system of the Roman empire, and turned that system against Christians and Jews in the first few centuries of our era. It went together with the systems of Catholic and Protestant theologians, especially in Spain, the Netherlands, Geneva, and England. It lent its services to the legitimist monarchical system of the holy alliance in Europe; it exercised the same function in the service of national socialism, and exercises it still today in the service of Marxism-Leninism.

Every system that makes a claim to exclusive power necessarily leads to some sort of inquisition. The late medieval theological system was no exception. It was even the most convincing confirmation of the proposition that *every* system claiming exclusive power brings with it a form of inquisition. For if a system built upon the basis of the religion of love proved capable of calling into being the Inquisition, what else can really be expected of other systems that rest upon such bases as "liberty, equality, and fraternity," "social justice," "scientific truth"? If even the principle of love was capable of being misled to the acts of the Inquisition, then inevitably every other principle can and must be even more decidedly so misled.

⊕

But what about the principle of *tolerance*? Does not tolerance, by virtue of its content and its nature, guarantee that a system based upon it will *not* result in an inquisition? Well, it was precisely on this principle of tolerance that the Roman system of law and religious politics was based. And yet it was precisely the Roman statesmen's concern to maintain this principle of tolerance that set in train the persecution of Christians and Jews! If it forms the basis of a system that claims exclusive power, the principle of tolerance is in effect nothing but *equilibrium*, i.e., a "balancing-out." If the share of one of the parts of the system of equilibrium becomes too great, a need therefore arises for forcible measures to balance-out the tendency "disturbing" the equilibrium: and so an inquisition commences in the name of tolerance! For instance, philosophers were persecuted and forcibly expelled from the city if their influence exceeded a "tolerable" dose. Thus, if it becomes the basis of a system claiming exclusive power, even the principle of tolerance is no exception to the rule—and it brings inquisition in its wake!

⊕

Whenever exclusive power is claimed for any system of thought (and, precisely, as a consequence of this claim), it drops out of the organic unity of what is human. It ceases to be a member of the life of the spirit, and becomes instead a sort of autonomous complex that sets itself in opposition to the total organism of the spiritual life of humanity. It is rather like a cancerous tumor in the body or a psychological complex in the soul.

A system claiming exclusive power becomes in actual fact a compulsive-neurotic complex in the spiritual life of humanity. This happened in the case of the theological system that once claimed exclusive power (and led finally to the Inquisition), even as it is happening today with the Marxist-Leninist system. In the total life of humanity, as we have said, both the theological system in the late middle ages and the Marxist-Leninist system of today are like a cancerous tumor in the body or a compulsive neurosis in the soul life of an individual person: neither wishes to serve the whole organism of human life, but to *rule* it.

The compulsive-neurotic effect of the theological system we have spoken of was expressed all too starkly in the late middle ages and in the early modern period. At that time, everyone lived in fear of this system. Every expression of thought was shadowed by the fear of having offended against the theological system. "Heresy" was the bogeyman that haunted people in schools, cloisters, castles, streets, and, in the end, even within the inner scene of the thoughts of individual people.

Courts of the Inquisition held their sessions day and night, filled with the conviction that the reigning theological system and the will of God were one and the same thing, and that human beings had no right to be mistaken. They forgot to draw the simplest conclusion from their own doctrine: that if God Himself tolerates the devil rather than annihilating him, He can certainly tolerate a poor human heretic or someone whose beliefs differ. The inquisitors themselves, however, lived under the coercion of the same complex of the sole power of the theological system, which compelled them to coerce all others as well. This sickness—in truth, this *madness*—made them blind and deaf to the most elementary truth of morality and religion: anything that does not happen as a result of freedom is morally valueless and has no religious substance.

The moral benightedness and mental derangement of

such people—who wished to sustain and further the religion of love by means of terror, torture, and burnings at the stake—can be explained in no other way than as a psychopathology, as symptoms of a true and actual psychic illness, whose consequence is no longer knowing what one is doing. Every fanaticism is a form and degree of neurotic compulsion and leads in the end to moral irresponsibility.

Even today there is a great deal more madness in the world than the number of cases treated medically. Stalin, for example, "knew" everything. He knew precisely how the two hundred million people whom he commanded should live and think. From the *system* of Marxism-Leninism, he knew better than they themselves what was beneficial to them and what was harmful. As a collective, the leadership of the communist party also "knows" better than all the rest of the world does. It knows what the nature of world history is and where it is leading; it knows that matter "secretes" consciousness and that the world's very substance wishes for communism; it knows everything and knows better about everything than the rest of the world does. How does this madness come about? Through the "possession" of consciousness by a system. Once one is in the power of a system, how easy it is to explain everything, to "know" everything!

Those in the Kremlin certainly do not know *more* than do thousands and thousands of other people in their own country, and in other countries, but they find it *easier* to arrive at unambiguous answers to any and all questions. The effort of the true labor of thinking has been removed from them: the machine, the system, does their thinking for them.

151

⊕

As regards the role of theology, it is much more a limb of the universal spiritual life of humanity now than a system claiming exclusive power—and is thus more an organic order, an ordered body of teaching, than a system formed to lord it over people by means of a network of incontrovertible concepts. Theology (or, more precisely, theologians) have also relinquished their claim to understand the world, humanity, and world history better than the representatives of all other methods of knowledge, individually or together. Put another way, the age of the world is no longer numbered at six thousand years, but at millions of years!

Today, all are free in theology to understand the creation narrative in Genesis as their own store of knowledge and conscience may dictate, on the condition that it should be taken *as* theology: not as a literary text but as revelation. The borderline between what is essential to religion and morality (i.e., dogma and its immediate consequences) and what is indifferent to religion and morality is drawn ever more sharply. It would not occur to any serious theologian today to dispute Albert Einstein's relativistic worldview, for example, in defense of Newton's physical worldview, in the way a position was once taken up in favor of the Ptolemaic system against the Copernican.

Even the results of modern research in depth psychology give occasion for theology to take up a position in their regard only insofar as they (or, more precisely, theoretical interpretations of these results) call into question the freedom of human beings and thus the basis of morality as such; or insofar as they treat religion not as revelation but as a psychologically-conditioned detour whereby the wishful dreams denied in life can be gratified. Theology would also have left socialism and communism to the economic scientists and politicians, had Marxism not broken into the theological domain and made atheism and materialism the basis of its system, and had communism not followed the path of the rule of terror and coercion.

In short, theology has relinquished its claim to sole mastery over the consciousness of human beings. By doing this, it has also won back its inner developmental possibilities. It is now free to learn from the total spiritual life of humanity, as well as to deepen its own spiritual resources. The paths to expansion and deepening lie open to theology. It is only a question of whether these paths will really be taken. As far as expansion is concerned, this is already well underway. Theology has learned and received much from the other sciences, particularly from historical research, archaeology, and linguistic scholarship. Comparative religion has brought with it a substantial expansion of theology's intellectual range and deepening of its concepts. Since the Bhagavad-Gita, the Upanishads, Taoist and Buddhist texts, and the Zohar have become accessible through translations, it is no longer possible to speak blithely in theology of "ignorant heathens." Indeed, it has become impossible even to speak in an abstract and superficial way of primitive natural religion (*religio naturalis*). Natural religion can no longer be conceived of merely as a kind of "Aristotelianism," as the bare acknowledgement of a World-Reason, or as the cultivation of the four cardinal virtues following from this: wisdom, courage, self-command, and justice.

⊕

The Virtues. The pre-Christian and extra-Christian religious life of humanity displays a richness that goes far beyond the bounds of an acknowledgement of a World-Reason and of the ethical ideals of the four cardinal virtues. For instance, the core virtue of Confucius, human warm-heartedness, goes far beyond the cardinal virtue of justice. It is a stage of the internalization of justice in the direction of love—and for this reason, it stands closer to the moral ideal of the religion of Israel than to the Platonic and Aristotelian worldview!

The Taoists' intimate inward occupation with the calm and modest highest Being of the world—Who nevertheless created and sustains all that is—likewise goes beyond the boundaries of an acknowledgement of the World-Reason. Spiritually, the Taoist is more closely related to such Christian mystics as Meister Eckhart, Tauler, Suso, and Boehme than to the spirit of Aristotelianism and Platonism, regardless of how noble and luminous the latter might be. In the teachers of Taoism, *the night speaks*; this is the calm, great night of the heavenly firmament and the deep abyss that speaks also in Eckhart and Boehme. By contrast, in the masters of Greek wisdom (with the exception of Heraclitus "the obscure"), *the day speaks*; and this is the sunlit, sharply-outlined day of consciousness. Thus, the *religio naturalis* of the ancients is not only the daylight tidings of World-Reason and of the four cardinal virtues, but the tidings of the night also:

> In ancient times, Bao Xi exercised true kingship over the Great Society in the following way. Looking upward to the heavens, he observed the signs in the heavens; and looking downwards, he observed the forms upon earth: the different forms of birds and animals and the universal agreement on the earth as a whole. He recognized in himself the way in which

individual things are connected in the universal. In this way, he invented the eight trigrams, in order to extend the divine sense of his spiritual power over everything, and in order to acknowledge the order of the natural properties of the entire world.

Thus reads the *Xici Zhuan* or *Commentary on the Appended Phrases* to the *Book of Changes* (*I Ching*). The "signs in the heavens" that Bao Xi observed were visible in the night sky, and the "different forms of birds and animals" on the earth were visible in daylight. The wisdom of Bao Xi contained the tidings of the night and the tidings of the day; it was the result of the harmony of the "waking" and "sleeping" layers of consciousness.

The "wise men from the East" of whom Matthew's gospel tells are the answer to the question of the nature of pre-Christian spirituality and its relationship to Christian revelation. The wise men were not prophets of Israel. They were, precisely, "wise men from the East": strangers in Israel and representatives of so-called heathendom. These heathen wise men were prepared in such a way that, without having witnessed the miraculous deeds of Jesus or heard his preaching, they sought him out to do him honor—a deed that many who were well-versed in the Scriptures and the prophets, and who had heard or could have heard Jesus's teaching, refused him.

The access possible today to the religious texts of the East has only strengthened the account given in Matthew's gospel of the wise men from the East, and made it more credible to non-theologians. For theologians who adopt the position that there are no "mere legends" in Scripture and must take all parts of scripture equally seriously, the account in Matthew's gospel is a sufficient and clear answer to the question: "Could the whole of humanity, with the sole exception of the people of Israel, have been held captive in the error and darkness of ignorance?"

If theologians of the twelfth and thirteenth centuries, particularly Albert the Great and Thomas Aquinas, answered this question with a "no" and (not without a difficult struggle) presented Aristotle and Plato as great intellectual figures from whom a Christian theologian might learn, it should be obvious to us today that what was then opened up as the path of learning from the past and from other cultural traditions, must now be taken further—and that this learning cannot rest content with Plato and Aristotle.

The Old Testament is still honored because it points out the path to the New Testament. But the wise men from the East assuredly also walked a path that led to the crib in Bethlehem, and thus to the New Testament. What was their path? What wisdom made them wise? What texts containing this wisdom belong to this path? Have we found them? And if so, do we hold them in such honor as we do the books and the wisdom of the Old Testament? If not, should we not seek them out in the spiritual life of the East? In considering the gospel account of the wise men of the East, is it not among the duties of the serious theologian to draw out *all* the consequences of this account?

A further expansion of theology on the order of what took place in the thirteenth century is unavoidable. The wisdom of the three wise men from the East can just as little be overlooked in our time as Plato and Aristotle could be overlooked then. This is all the more pressing because a growing number of people not only detect the presence of this wisdom but are gradually discovering and coming to know its essential characteristics. Much "gold" wisdom, "frankincense" of God's honor, and "myrrh" of the recollective cultivation of the past—the three gifts of the wise men from the East—has already been recovered from the treasure troves of the Middle East, India, and China.

India's great ideas concerning the moral world order, *karma* and *dharma* (the moral law *in the world* and the moral law *within us*) cannot simply be rejected on the grounds that they are not expressly formulated in the Bible. We need to consider that the whole make-up of the Bible rests upon the fact that there was a Fall, that the fate of humanity was determined by this *moral* event, and that another *moral* event or *moral* deed (the sacrificial death on Golgotha) introduced a far-reaching transformation in the universal destiny of humanity. True, we cannot say that the Bible (the Old Testament and the New Testament) offers a direct formulation of the moral law prevailing in world history, but we can say that it graphically *illustrates* the reality of this law's operation.

If the methods and findings of disciplines far removed from religion (such as archaeology, philology, botany, and zoology) are not scorned in Biblical studies, why, in order to understand the Bible better, should we not make use of the law of the moral world order, the law of *karma*, which belongs entirely to the domain proper of religious concerns? Is it because this would mean a rebirth of gnosis?

⊕

Gnosis. Knowledge (for gnosis *means* knowledge), however, cannot be denied in principle if we wish to be pupils of the Master who commanded us: "Know the truth, and the truth shall make you free." Such a denial can be valid only with respect to a particular *kind* of knowledge, that is, historical gnosis—the teachings of the Ophites, Marcionites, Manichaeans, Valentinians, Basildeans, and so on. There are indeed good reasons for rejecting these teachings; but does conceding this mean licence is thereby granted to reject as valueless or erroneous humanity's religious intuitions or insights—which happen to have seen the light of day outside the cycle set in motion by the Judeo-Christian traditions?

Alongside false gnosis can there not also exist a true gnosis, just as scientific errors exist alongside true scientific achievements? We cannot reject science outright just because there have also been, and still are, scientific errors. Should gnosis, then, as the striving for deeper insight into religious truths, be judged any differently? Should this whole area of interest be condemned solely on the grounds that once upon a time there were erroneous gnostic teachings?

Heresy does not originate in knowledge of religious truths, but in ignorance or insufficient knowledge of them. Arius's knowledge in this regard was, for example, time-bound and incapable of raising itself up from the succession of temporal events to timeless being in eternity. He could conceive of the becoming of the Son out of the Father only as a temporal event, as a succession. The consequence of this incapacity was the doctrine that Christ was a created being, even if the highest created being. The Arians could not grasp the birth of the Son "before all time" (*ante omnia saecula*) in eternity: "Light from light, true God from true God, begotten, not made, of one being with the Father" (*Deus verus de Deo vero, lumen de lumine, natus non factus*). They lacked the higher gnosis of Christian revelation.

The conflict between Arius and Athanasius (or between Arianism and Athanasianism) is by its very nature a conflict

158

between a superficial and a deeper insight into the mystery of Christianity, a conflict between a rationalistically limited gnosis and a higher gnosis. And the so-called Athanasian Creed, which proclaims the saving truths of Christianity in the light of the eternal Trinity with both wondrous clarity and beauty, is the result of the victory of the higher gnosis over rationalism's assault upon it. Arius and Athanasius were both believers. Strength of belief was not in question in the great conflict of the fourth century, but the respective *insight* into the content of the faith that each party confessed. Arius did not deny the gospel or the Bible. He only *understood* them in a different way than Athanasius did.

What goes for Arius also goes, in principle, for all who have been deemed heresiarchs. Thus, as men lacking almost any sense for gnosis, Calvin and Luther were not representatives of the higher gnosis either, even though they were both markedly people of faith. Indeed, in the last analysis their concern was to extirpate gnosis, root and branch, from the Christian religion, and to reshape Christianity into a completely gnosis-free matter of pure faith—to "reform" it.

Luther. Luther's doctrine that faith alone saves, and that everything else is the action of grace, meant at the same time not only a renunciation of the principle of actually *practicing* a religion ("the kingdom of heaven suffereth violence"), and thus of the practice of the rosary, spiritual exercises in the sense of meditation and contemplation, the examination of one's conscience, confession, the vows of poverty, obedience, and chastity—but it was also tantamount to renouncing the principle of gnosis that underlies this practice. It meant renouncing the principle of striving to become worthy of suprasensory and suprarational illumination and insight by means of preparatory instruction.

In Lutheranism there is no spiritual instruction in fasting, the examination of conscience, penitence, prayer, meditation, and contemplation. There is only theological training. And if there were (and perhaps still are) individual mystics and gnostics, even among Lutherans such as the shoemaker from Görlitz, Jakob Boehme, their experiences and insights are more the result of a personal striving for gnosis than of Lutheran teaching and religious praxis. Jakob Böhme has more in common with Meister Eckhart on the one hand, and with the alchemic-hermetic movement on the other, than he does with Luther. His doctrine of the *Ungrund*, to which Schelling in the nineteenth century and Berdyaev in the twentieth were so greatly indebted, is closer in spirit to Meister Eckhart's doctrine of the "Godhead," and indeed to the Jesuit mystic Angelus Silesius, than to Luther, whose faith was in the words of Scripture alone. Protestant mystics (Moravians and Quakers included) are phenomena related to the universal human need for mysticism and gnosis. In them this need broke free from the depths of the consciousness to which it had been confined, and became dominant.

Calvin. Calvin's teaching is also the outcome of a surgical operation on the body of Christianity. It is the remnant of that body left after the denial of hierarchy (laymen, priests, bishops, archbishops...) and of free will, and thus also of the path of spiritual instruction and the stages along this path—that is, a denial of the principle of gnosis. It is just as "democratic," universally intelligible, and fatalistic as Islam.

Calvinism is really an Islamized form of Christianity. It contains no contradictions. It is logically consistent. It is consistent to say: "If God is omniscient and omnipotent, He knows everything and can do everything. If He knows everything, He also determines the future down to the last detail. Consequently, He also knows who will be saved and who will be damned. From all eternity He has elected some souls to salvation and other souls to damnation. None of this can be changed, because God has determined it thus."

These inferences from God's omniscience and omnipotence are illuminating. But they are nonetheless completely false insofar as they sever God's omniscience and omnipotence from their connection with His all-embracing love! Omniscience and omnipotence *in the service of love* mean something quite different from omniscience and omnipotence without love. Calvin lacked the higher gnosis of the mystery of love, which became in the crucifix both a fact and an emblem. The crucifix, the crucified Son who is one with the Father, is not the emblem of omnipotence and omniscience, but of a love that has *renounced* omnipotence and omniscience. At the same time, it is also the emblem of the freedom of the people who stand at the foot of the cross. For by not compelling, but by *renouncing* His omniscient omnipotence, God gives His creatures freedom. Conversely, by giving creatures freedom, God limits His omniscient omnipotence—that is, He is crucified. If this were not the case, if Christ were not crucified love but ruling omnipotence, the horrors of national socialism and communism would be God's work. God would be directly responsible for all evil, for everything wicked. This, however, would be the greatest conceivable slander upon and blasphemy against God.

Calvin lacked the gnosis of the crucified God, the gnosis of the mystery of love and freedom, just as many other people, adhering to a wide variety of religious confessions, give evidence of lacking this gnosis whenever they speak of the governance of the Almighty in history—for by speaking in this way they are really only repeating the mocking cry of the hangman at the cross: "Save thyself"!

⊕

The higher gnosis that all heresiarchs lacked was the gnosis of the mystery of love. They had no "ear" for the meaning and significance of love. Arius could not discern the simultaneous unity *and* distributedness of the Father and the Son because he lacked insight into the unity of the diverse in love. The Monophysites could not understand the unity of the *two* natures—the divine and human—in Jesus Christ because they lacked a sense for the unity of the diverse in love. The Docetists denied the reality of Christ's sufferings on the cross because they held him to be a divinity who merely *appeared* human, because they lacked knowledge of the unity of the diverse in love. Pelagius asserted the primacy of human works in bringing about salvation because he could not comprehend the unity of the diverse, of works and grace, in love. Luther asserted the primacy of grace and held all human works to be vain because he lacked insight into the unity of the diverse in love. Calvin denied free will and affirmed providence alone because the meaning of the mystery of the crucifixion eluded him.

In practice, defective understanding of love usually brings with it *lovelessness*. Thus one can only rightly understand and value the idea and the reality of the Universal Church on the basis of the higher gnosis of love. The teach-

162

ing that the Church is the mystical body of Christ (*corpus Christi mysticum*) is gnostic through and through. Without an appeal to the higher gnosis (i.e., being confined to the limited means of reason and sensuous experience), this teaching is senseless. If it is taken as it is meant, however (i.e., as a spiritual and moral truth of faith), it becomes an unconquerable source of light. "I am in the Father, and ye in me, and I in you" is the formula for the Church.

Those who understand this will never do anything that could harm the unity of the Church. Out of love for the Church, they would rather put up with injustice towards themselves than offend against the unity of the Church. The heresiarchs, however, lacked this love. They founded their own communities, their own "churches," whenever they had a different opinion. Their own opinion was dearer to them than the unity of the Church. When Luther uttered the much-praised and marveled-at sentence, "Here I stand, I can do no other, so help me God," it never occurred to anyone to doubt his sincerity and honesty. We, however, can scarcely avoid some skepticism regarding his love of humanity and his sense of historical responsibility. When he uttered these words, did he think of the consequences they would have for the unity of the Church, for the unity of Christian humanity, for family life, for children and the dying, for missionaries in foreign countries, for the prayer life of individuals, for the remembrance of the dead, for the veneration of the saints, for the veneration of the Mother of God, for the ideals of future generations? "*I* can do no other..." he says. Is the *I*, and what it thinks it "can do" at this particular hour of this particular day, the highest court and highest source of wisdom? Is the *I* incapable of learning anything further? Did Luther himself not have the experience of the mutability of "personal convictions" in a way that might have led him to approach the "personal conviction" of this particular hour with more caution and in a less absolute manner? When Luther was an ascetic Augustinian monk, was he less "personally convinced" than he was later, when he stood before the *Reichstag*?

These questions can be answered in various ways, but asking them is justified if we have in mind not only personal honesty but also the sense of historical responsibility. This is so, because those for whom the Church is the mystical body of Christ, for whom it *actually* is that body, will always place historical responsibility above any given "personal conviction." They will always do this because humanity is for them "humanity," and not "*I* plus the others."

⊕

Let us look at some of the consequences of Luther's deed, not in the political realm, but in that of religious life itself. How great is the impoverishment his deed brought about in this realm! How many sources of inspiration, how many ways of expressing love, have been overthrown! How many models and ideals have faded and fallen into oblivion!

Thus, the rich inner and ennobling life of the veneration and venerating knowledge of the Virgin Mother has been overthrown, and with it, half the wealth of the religious life of the soul has been lost. For the most precious experiences we ever receive in our life on earth are those of maternal and paternal love. The abolition of the heavenly model and archetype of maternal love means the same impoverishment for the religious life as does the early loss of a mother in a human life. A child who knows only its father is poorer than the child who knew and loved both parents. A like impoverishment took place in the Protestant part of the Christian world.

The countless memorial candles of the veneration of the saints were extinguished also. We do not forget what we love. Love is also remembrance, recollection, and commemoration. The Church daily remembers those who through their life or death revealed something great, something worthy of veneration and of continual remembrance. The saints are the treasury of the moral historical experience of humanity. At the same time, they are the soul's school of preparation for the divine. For how can anyone unworthy of the divine in its partial revelations be worthy of the plenitude of the divine? How can anyone who does not treasure the holy when it is revealed in the person whom they see, really treasure the holy in God, whom they do not see?

The treasury of historical recollection has been impoverished. The wealth of inspiration, of wonder, and of deeper knowledge that can be acquired from the life histories of such saints as St Teresa of Avila, St Ignatius Loyola, St Francis, St Xavier, St Catherine of Siena, St John Vianney, has disappeared in Protestant religious life. The Bible, the Patriarchs, the Kings and Prophets of the Old Testament are known, the figures of the New Testament likewise. But then comes an abrupt fifteen-hundred-year-long gap in moral and religious remembrance. It is from this religious and moral vacuum that Luther and Calvin emerge. There, religious and moral remembrance comes to an end.

The gap opened in this way is filled with politicians, generals, philosophers, and poets. This, however, is *culture*, not religion. It is not the history of dealings with God (as is the

Bible), nor of the continuation of that history (as are the lives of the saints), but the history of human beings for their own sake. It is good, at any rate, that man without God is at least still remembered, for a time may come when only economic relationships and technological progress will be remembered...

Even our relationship with the dead has retreated to the lowest possible intensity as a result of Protestantism. We bid farewell to the dead, and leave their further fate to God's grace. But can we be sure we have thereby done everything that might serve and help the dead? *Are we permitted* to be sure that the dead *no longer* need anything after they have drawn their last breath, or that we can no longer assist them in any way? That the work of compassion and love is at an end once the mortal remains have been buried? That death is an ending? However this might be, there is more compassion in praying for the dead than in not praying for them; and there is more love in continual active prayer for the dead than there is if we leave them to their own fate. It is an impoverishment of the moral and religious life to limit the life of prayer to the circle of the living.

But even the life of prayer that restricts itself to the living alone is impoverished if we reject the principle of intercession. If we do not wish to say, with Cain, "Am I my brother's keeper?" but to strive instead to *become* our brother's keeper, his protector, it follows that our prayer develops into an intercession. The meaning of intercession for the living and the dead, for friends, enemies, and apostates, for the untaught and the unteachable, can be seen with particular clarity in the conversation the devout Moses has with the LORD. After the people of Israel had fallen away and prayed to the golden calf, the LORD proclaimed his decision to destroy them and allow a new people to come into being from the posterity of Moses. Then Moses puts himself between the LORD and his people; he stands before the LORD and protects his people with his own life, saying "then destroy me too, together with my people." And the people were spared for Moses's sake.

The meaning and practical significance of prayer is that we identify ourselves with the other, that we pray and act in the name of the other. This is also the meaning of the request for intercession, for example the request "Holy Mary, pray for us!" This request, uttered for so many centuries in the West and the East, has resulted in an experience cultivated and celebrated especially in the East in early Russia. It is summed up in the image of the "mantle of the Mother of God" (in Russian, *Pokrov Bogomateri*).[1] This "protecting mantle" is the answer to the request for intercession. It is the protecting tabernacle in which gather all those with whose fate the heavenly queen identifies—the mantle of the heavenly maternal heart...

⊕

All these things belong to gnosis, to the knowledge that can be had when the understanding kneels. It is not enough to kneel physically. The understanding, reason itself, is also to learn to kneel. Reason is not to be excluded or put to sleep,

---

[1] *Pokrov Bogomateri* is also the name of a Christian feast of the Mother of God (Theotokos) celebrated in Eastern Orthodox and Byzantine Catholic Churches on the first day of October. *Pokrov* has a complex meaning. First of all, it refers to a cloak or mantle; but it also means protection or intercession. For this reason, the name of the feast is variously translated as The Veil of Our Lady, The Protecting Veil of the Theotokos, The Feast of the Intercession, or The Feast of the Holy Protection.

but to kneel in wakeful brightness before what is higher than it. It is not itself to speak, but to silently hearken. It is not to create its own forms of thinking, but to become as smooth as a mirror, and reflect. The original and true meaning of "speculation" (from *speculum*, a mirror) was precisely that of reason in a state of mirroring—reason that does not spin a web out of itself, but hearkens and mirrors.

When in a state where no gnosis takes place (and that is even hostile to gnosis), reason produces either heresies, or else formally and legalistically maintained theological systems. Heresies result from a lack of insight into the mysteries of love. Arid, formalistic theological systems are intellectual commentaries on the original—commentaries that attempt to translate a gnosis alien to them into their own intellectual language. This can and may happen; it is indeed the proper task of theology as a science. But it may only happen when the original is itself understood not intellectually but gnostically. There must be a living gnosis standing behind the theology. Theologians are not to draw formal inferences from formal propositions, but to draw their inferences from the truths they know in a substantive manner. This means they are not to apply the method of the juristic exposition of a law, but the method of *symbolism*. Just as Christ himself produced no doctrinal system, but spoke mostly through parables, so theology ought to follow its Master and translate its gnosis into the language of intellect in the same way symbols are interpreted. The intellect will only refrain from doing violence to the higher gnosis (the gnosis, for example, that forms the basis of the Athanasian Creed) if used symbolically. An example of the juridical and formal, rather than the symbolic and substantive, method in theology can be found in the controversy over the *filioque*, which supplied a theological basis for the schism of the Eastern Church in the eleventh century.

Since it is said in John's gospel (14:26) that the Father will send "the Comforter, which is the Holy Spirit," theologians of the Greek East insist that the sentence of the creed concerning the Holy Spirit, *et in Spiritum Sanctum, Domnium et vivificantem, qui ex Patre Filioque procedit,* should, accordingly, read *qui ex Patre procedit* (that is, omitting the *filioque*). The West was accused of heresy for not allowing the Spirit to proceed from the Father alone, as is explicitly stated in John's gospel, but rather from the Father *and* the Son. Now, *formally,* the Eastern theologians are right, since this is indeed stated in John's gospel, and since the more ancient versions of the creed do not seem to have contained the *filioque*. But how does this question stand substantively?

The same speech of Christ[2] whence we have the sentence about the procession of the Holy Spirit also contains the sentences: "I am in the Father, and the Father in me"; "If I go not away, the Comforter will not come unto you; but if I depart, I will send him unto you"; and "All things that the Father hath are mine." In other words, this same speech contains sentences emphasizing the *unity* of the Father and the Son. Indeed, the thought is there expressed that the Son goes to the Father *in order* to send the Holy Spirit. Were he not to go to the Father, the Holy Spirit would not come. Which is to say that, on His own, the Father will not send the Spirit. In any case, what is essential is that Father and Son are one ("all mine are thine, and thine are mine").

Considered substantively, then, it is entirely justified to say that the Holy Spirit proceeds from the Father and from

[2] John's gospel, chapters 13–17. VT.

169

the Son, just as it is justified to say that the Spirit proceeds from the Father. This is also the Catholic Church's standpoint today: both versions of the creed are simultaneously valid, and the Catholics of the Eastern Rite use the creed without the *filioque.*

This controversy is quite telling, in that it signifies a conflict between insight into the nature of the thing, and insistence on the literal words of the text—a conflict between a higher gnosis and mere textual learning.

⊕

What is gnosis? It is the deeper insight produced by immersion in the objects of faith. Thinking through, feeling through, and practicing the objects of faith leads to a deepening of our insights into them and of our conception of them. Such insights and conceptions are no other than the dimension of depth in which gnosis grows in the soil of faith. Thus one can believe, for example, that God created the world, without having insight also into the sequence and the stages of the acts of the Creation as they are depicted in Genesis. But if the composition, context, and meaning of the six days' labor enter into our consciousness, gnosis arises. But it arises only on the basis of faith; indeed it *is* a growing certainty of faith, since anyone who takes the Creation story of Genesis in a merely literary or historical or even psychological way will never gain *insight* into its deeper content, will never attain to gnosis.

Gnosis presupposes faith. Faith alone is able to bring about the seriousness, the concentration, and the absorption necessary for gnosis. Indeed, what occasion would one have had to immerse oneself for many years in the terse sentences of the account of the Creation in the Bible, had one not understood them, from the first, as providing an *actual* history of the Creation?

From out of fire comes light; from out of faith comes gnosis. Fire, however, requires air and combustible material in order to burn. The air that the fire of faith needs is freedom; the combustible material it needs is everything within us that we know ought to be overcome. Freedom and expiation, or voluntary expiation, is the element in which faith catches fire. No one, and nothing, can extort faith, since it can only live in and from freedom; and self-overcoming (the overcoming of everything mechanical, automatic, and habitual in us) is the process of the transformation of the combustible material in the fire. And this fire radiates light. Thus does gnosis arise.

Theologians have to do with the deepest matters. How is it possible for them to seek immersion without depth?[3] How long is the path of immersion in the concept, in the idea, in the ideal, and in the nature of God? That is, how long is the path whose signposts are the biblical names of God, the path that leads through the names *Adonai, Yahweh Sabaoth, Elion, Elohim, El, Ehiyeh* to *Ab*, the "Father" of the New Testament? These names contain a world of knowledge of God. Their stages and aspects should mean more for theologians than historical-linguistic or aesthetic and poetic problems.[4] Is it really theology when, in a three-volume work written in Latin, the *Synopsis theologiae dogmaticae* by A. Tanquerey SS (a work prescribed for the use

---

[3] Immersion (*Ver-tiefung*); depth (*Tiefe*).

[4] See the author's *Proclamation on Sinai: Covenant and Commandments* (Brooklyn, NY: Angelico Press, 2022), "Interlude: The Use of God's Name in Meditation," 63–80.

of seminaries), the following is said of the "names" of God?

> *El* is regarded as the oldest name which the Semites
> gave to the highest being; it is occasionally used by
> the writers of Holy Scripture in the plural, *Elohim*; it
> does not follow from this, however, that the Hebrews
> were originally polytheists, since this name is accom-
> panied by words in the singular describing its quali-
> ties and activities. This is a case of the *plurale
> majestativum*, which indicates the plurality of the
> qualities of the divine being (*indicans in divina essentia
> multiplicem esse virtutem*). . . . From this it can proba-
> bly be concluded that *El* and *Elohim* designate "He
> who is mighty" (*eum qui potens est*).
>
> *Eloah* means the same, in the opinion of some, and
> derives from the Arabic *aliha*, meaning "astonished,
> seized with trembling" (*stupit, pavore perculsus est*), so
> that its meaning would be "the Lord who excites
> trembling" (*terribilis Dominis*).
>
> *El-Elyon*, or simply *Elyon*, means the same as "the
> most high" (*altissimus*), and is the name with which
> Melchizedek designates the supreme being (Genesis
> 14:18).
>
> *El-Shaddai*, which in the view of many derives from
> the Hebrew word *shasah* (zealous, powerful: *vehe-
> mens, potens*), means "the Almighty" (*omnipotens*),
> since He expresses his power in an extraordinary
> way; according to others, however, this name derives
> from *shad* (breast: *ubera*) and indicates plenitude or
> fertility.

Jehovah, which in the opinion of scholars should be pronounced *Yahweh*, is derived from the stem *hawah* (he was: *fuit*), and many are of the opinion that it denotes the being whose characteristic quality is *being* (*esse*) without any limitations, or which possesses the fullness of being. However, several modern experts are of the opinion that *Yahweh* is a causative form, and accordingly means "that causes being," or Creator (*creator*). . . .

Adonai means the same as "Lord" (*Dominus*), and indicates God's supreme rule (Genesis 15:2).

Jehovah Sabaoth first occurs in Kings 1:3 and is translated in the Vulgate as "Lord of hosts" (*dominus exercituum*). With this name God is addressed not only as Lord of the established lands of Israel, but also as Lord of the heavenly bodies and the angels. . . .

It thus follows from what we have said of the particular names of God that God is depicted in Scripture as *powerful* (*potens*) and *strong* (*fortis*), endowed with *many abilities* in the unity of his being; as the *highest being*, whose sight brings human beings to *tremble*; as the *all-highest*, whom all are to serve; as the *almighty*, whose works tower over the laws of nature; as the *being* who possesses the fullness of being, and who is the *cause* of the being of other beings; as the *Lord* who rules over the world and governs it . . . who rules the *heavenly bodies* and who has *angels for ministers*. . . .[5]

Thus far Tanquerey on the names of God. What is said

---

[5] Based on the author's translation from Adolphe Tanquerey's *Synopsis theologiae dogmaticae specialis*, Band 1, Baltimore, 1894, 100–2.

here about the names of God precisely corresponds in its content, scope, and level to what linguistics and historical research combined would have to say on this subject. In what, then, does the authentic contribution to theology consist here? Ought it not to consist in some deeper insight into the nature of the names of God, following on from this philological and historical preparatory work?

Here we have an example from the domain of theology in which the necessity of a knowledge that goes beyond science (the necessity of gnosis, that is) is clear to see. It is not enough to know the translation of these names, or to know where and how many times they occur in Scripture. For if it is said in John's gospel (17:6) that "I have manifested thy name unto the men which thou gavest me out of the world," and later (17:26) that "I have declared unto them thy name, and will declare it: that the love wherewith thou hast loved me may be in them, and I in them," then it is obviously a matter, not of a name that can be explained philologically and historically, but of a new stage in the revelation of God and in the knowledge of this revelation. It is a matter, that is, of a higher gnosis. And just as the name that is spoken of in John's gospel has the meaning of the revelation and knowledge of the divine Being, so the other names that occur in the Bible have a similar meaning.

In the Old Testament, for example, the tetragrammaton, the holy name YHVH (Yahweh), was taken so seriously that it could not be spoken. Even today its proper pronunciation can only be conjectured, because the vowel points supplied in the Masoretic text for YHVH (which led to the reading "Jehovah") are those for the name *Adonai*, LORD—the name that was spoken wherever YHVH was found in the text.

Another example of the sacredness and revelatory value

174

of the divine name in the Old Testament is afforded by the particular circumstances under which the divine name "I AM THAT I AM" (Exodus 3:14) was revealed to Moses in the burning bush. The French philosopher Étienne Gilson set such a high value on the significance of this event for the spiritual history of humanity that he argued it was the principle of all later Christian philosophy:

> Exodus lays down the principle from which hence-
> forth the whole of Christian philosophy will be sus-
> pended. From this moment it is understood once and
> for all that the proper name of God is Being and
> that . . . this name denotes his very essence.[6]

Indeed, as Gilson further describes, the name *ego sum qui sum* was considered as the highest of God's names by St Ephrem of Nisibis, St Gregory Nazianzen, St Cyril of Alexandria, and later by St Hilary of Poitiers, St Thomas Aquinas, and St Bonaventure—that is, for a timespan of nearly a millennium. In the Jewish Kabbalah, too, this name was awarded the highest rank, that of the "crown" (*keter*) among the ten names of God.

All these Fathers and Doctors of the Church, and Kabbalists (e.g., Isaac Luria and Chaim Vital in the sixteenth and early seventeenth century),[7] like Étienne Gilson in the twentieth century, regarded the name of God "I AM THAT I AM" not as a philological problem, but as matter for meditation on a deeper level upon the nature of God, as matter for insight and gnosis. The other biblical names of God

---

[6] *The Spirit of Mediæval Philosophy*, trsl A.H.C Downes (New York: Charles Scribner's Sons, 1940), 51.

[7] The author's manuscript mistakenly describes Isaac Luria (1534–1572) and Chaim Vital (1543–1620) as fourteenth-century Kabbalists.

deserve the same degree of attention as that given the name "I AM THAT I AM," and should serve as matter upon which every serious theologian should meditate. For theology has God at the center of its whole concern, and the highest object also puts the highest demands on those who concern themselves with it. We cannot, however, do justice to these demands if we do not go beyond philological-historical, juridical, and psychological efforts. If we do go beyond them, however, we are taking the step from science to gnosis.

⊕

Where exactly does the border lie between theology, philosophy (or philosophy of religion), mysticism, and gnosis? Where, for example, is St Thomas Aquinas a theologian and where a philosopher? Is Meister Eckhart only a mystic, rather than being a theologian or a philosopher at all? Or is he a gnostic? Is the "existentialist philosopher" Nikolai Berdyaev (who regards St Augustine and Blaise Pascal as true existentialist philosophers, but not Heidegger or Jaspers) a gnostic, since he speaks of the *Ungrund* of nothingness,[8] from which spring freedom and evil? Or is he a philosopher of religion, since he has said a great deal about God, creation, freedom, immortality, heaven, and hell? Or is he even a theologian, since all these questions belong to the realm of theology?

I suggest that we not trouble ourselves with the question of how to classify those who are concerned with metaphysical matters. For every person who "cannot live by bread alone" is in principle at once a philosopher, theologian,

---

[8] In the manner of Jacob Boehme.

mystic, and gnostic. Every prayer is the practical "mysticism" of a dealing with God. Every insight into the nature of this dealing is "gnosis." All the thoughts we may have about these matters insofar as we hold to the teaching handed down by the Church, are "theology." And if we do not hold to the teaching of the Church in these matters, we are engaged in "philosophy." Many who outwardly appear to be professed "philosophers" or "theologians" are secretly carrying on mysticism and gnosis. We must not forget that even Sir Isaac Newton wrote commentaries on the Book of Revelation.

Since we are concerned here with the paths to personal certainty, whether followed in secret or in public, i.e., with the paths into the metaphysical questions that religion, theology, philosophy, mysticism, and gnosis have in common (i.e., with the *questions of humanity*), it may be permitted to regard those who follow all these paths as devout *persons*, and as such to take their advice. When it was said earlier that a theologian who takes the divine names as matter for meditation is taking a step "from science to gnosis," this in no way means that such a theologian has become unfaithful to the task and methods of theology. It is only that, as a *person*, another layer of consciousness is now active in him also, which may perhaps *to him personally* bring great enrichment and an increased certainty, but which in theology may perhaps at first only find expression in a few terse phrases.

Thus it may happen that a theologian who has made the "divine names" into matter for meditation, and who *for himself* has found in them a world of content, will draw only two methodologically justified consequences in their regard with respect to his outer engagement with the discipline of theology: he will set out the "divine names" in a particular sequence (one that is indeed grounded in what is essential, but is formally a matter of indifference); and he will follow this with a recommendation (one that is indeed easy to justify theologically) to make these names into matter for meditation. This result will certainly seem a small contribution to the field of theology, but its *significance* can hardly be underestimated if we recall that a sequence of the "divine names" grounded in what is essential can exert a stimulating and awakening influence, and that the use of the "divine names" thus grounded as matter for meditation can lead us beyond the initial literal sense of these names and to progress in the direction of deepening them. This means, however, that we are now taking the "divine names" as symbols, as an "intellectual iconography" of God. With this there opens up for us the beginning of a path of ever intensifying personal certainty, whose end is hardly to be foreseen.

A deepening labor on the names of God as symbols, or as intellectual icons of God, was in the past probably very often undertaken and performed. I am familiar with an example of such labor from the past that, apart from its value as a stimulant and its gnostic content, can do good service towards further illustrating the labor on and with symbols to the end of *personal* deepening, since the claim to scientificity, i.e., to universal validity and compelling necessity of method, is alien to symbolism—both as such, and in particular as regards the labor on and with the "divine names." The example I have in mind is the "tree" of the *sefirot* in the Kabbalah.

Since the "divine names" bear an organic connection with the whole field of kabbalistic symbolism, it will be impossible not to devote a chapter of its own to this topic.

VI

The Tree of the *Sefirot* and the Names of God

WHEREAS THE TEMPLES OF EGYPT, MESOPOTA-
mia, Phoenicia, and Greece were places where
images and statues of the gods were seen and
worshipped, the Temple in Jerusalem was the
place where the invisible God, without image or shape, was
worshipped. Instead, a scroll containing the *written word* of
God was brought out and read aloud in the Holy of Holies
of the Temple. For the ancient Israelites, the written word
replaced the holy images and forms of neighboring peoples.
They learned to worship the sublime and the divine in the
word, not in the image or form. *Names* became for them
sacred symbols, just as statues were the sacred symbols of
the so-called heathens.

The forty years of wandering in the wilderness were a
preparation that meant more than merely renouncing the
advantages of sedentary life: those years were at the same
time the period of "wandering in the wilderness" in the
sense of being absent from cultic places, temples, festivals,
and images of the gods. In other words, those wandering
years represented the process of breaking with the whole
Egyptian way of life. That this was not easy can be seen from
the fact that they relapsed into worshipping the golden calf.

The result of the discipline of the people of Israel, a discipline of the impossibility of representing or imagining God (begun by Moses and continued by the judges and the prophets) was a correspondingly stronger concentration of attention on the word, in particular upon the written word of Holy Scripture. This concentration on the written word was the precondition for the development of a "scriptural scholarship" that went into the most minute details of Scripture and of the soil in which such scholarship grew. It was, however, also the soil in which the gnostic and mystical immersion in the written word of Scripture—the Kabbalah[1]—took its origin and flourished. The *literal* interpretation of Scripture led to the development of scriptural scholarship, which later became so-called Talmudic scholarship. The *symbolic* interpretation of Scripture, on the other hand, led to the development of the Kabbalah, which was still playing a leading role in the spiritual life of the religious communities of the Hasidim in Eastern Europe only a short while ago.

The Kabbalah is universally known as the "secret teaching of the Jews." This idea of the Kabbalah is at once correct and mistaken. It is *correct* insofar as the Kabbalah was unobtrusively cultivated and handed down within religious Jewry for many centuries: the *Sefer Yetzirah* (the *Book of Creation* of the Kabbalists) is already quoted in the Talmud (that is, by the fifth century AD at the latest). It is *incorrect*, however, insofar as by "secret teaching" we understand a teaching "kept secret" or "made into a secret." The "secret" element in this "secret teaching" consisted, and consists still, in the fact that it did not wish to be a universally valid

---

[1] The more precise transliteration is *Qabbalah*. VT

system that would replace the orthodox teaching of the Jews, but was directed instead to *individuals*. It withheld nothing from individuals. It did *not* wish to be a "law" directed, not to individuals, but to the community, to the collective. It is directed to individuals who have needs that it can satisfy, or that it believes it can satisfy. The concerns of individuals are not, however, in themselves "secret": they are, rather, *intimate*. In this sense, it would be more accurate to describe the Kabbalah not as a secret teaching, but as an *intimate* teaching.

Here the manuscript ends